The Saudi Kingdom

The Saudi Kingdom

Between the Jihadi Hammer
and the Iranian Anvil

Ali al Shihabi

THE CHOIR PRESS

First published in the United Kingdom in 2015 by

The Choir Press

ISBN 978-0-909300-78-1

Contents

CHAPTER 1

The Kingdom Today

The Kingdom of Saudi Arabia today faces a multiplicity of domestic and external threats. Should this kingdom, often described as the "central bank" of the global oil industry, fall to an external attack or internal revolution, the impact on what remains today of the Arab nation-state order and the knock-on effect on global oil prices will be incalculable.

Today, radical jihadi ideology calling for the overthrow of the House of Saud is spreading among frustrated Saudi youth who are increasingly politicized and radicalized by social media and also militarized by fighting in Iraq, Syria, and Yemen. This threat becomes all the more potent as jihadis arrive on the kingdom's northern border with Iraq and on its southern border with Yemen. At the same time, a hostile Iran, with aggressive political ambitions in the Middle East, tightens its hold over Shia-led Iraq, as spreading sectarianism provides Iran and its Iraqi allies with increasing influence and sway over the disgruntled Shia community of Saudi Arabia's oil-producing Eastern Province and also over the recently empowered Houthi Shia militia in Yemen.

Arabian elites live on islands of conspicuous wealth and

prosperity surrounded by an ocean of poor, covetous, and hostile people. These are the millions of underprivileged Arabs in Yemen, Jordan, Iraq, and the Levant; the masses of economically distressed Iranians; and a not insubstantial number of less-privileged Saudi citizens. While not as desperately poor as their neighbors, these Saudis are increasingly demanding a "fair" share of what they consider to be *their* oil wealth while accusing their rulers of taking a disproportionate share for themselves. Such envy and resentment is fueling the growing hostility that is enveloping the Saudi ruling order.

Despite these mounting dangers, the kingdom continues to be led by rulers who are distracted by internal family politics and are seemingly oblivious to the extent of their vulnerabilities. For their security, they continue to depend on their traditional alliance with the elders of the Wahhabi establishment and on US military protection combined with the occasional financial largesse that they dispense both to their neighbors and their own people. Regardless of some noises to the contrary, their actions show that they do not fully appreciate that times have changed, their people's expectations and political awareness have increased, their enemies have multiplied and become more dangerous, and the United States may no longer be willing or even able to protect them as before.

Saudi rulers do not see any need to adapt their ruling model to cope with this increasingly complex and dangerous environment. Their model of a huge, self-absorbed, and generously provided-for royal family exerting unconstrained and absolute power over more than twenty-eight million people is simply not sustainable in this day and age. Al Saud's success, so far, in beating the odds that have always been stacked up against them has numbed their senses to the shifting ground they stand on. While today they probably retain the power, the resources, and enough prestige and legitimacy with the majority of their people to be able to succeed with political reform, every day they postpone introducing such reform brings the day of reckoning inevitably closer.

Stakeholders in Saudi stability watch developments in the kingdom in a somewhat complacent manner, not exercising their imagination sufficiently to consider and explore the risks, parameters, and ultimate implications of a potential collapse of the Saudi monarchy.

The United States, while rapidly acquiring energy self-sufficiency and increasingly fatigued by its involvement in the Middle East, remains the only stakeholder with any possible influence on the Saudi monarchy, yet it has hardly expended any effort to push for political reform in the kingdom beyond its traditional call for "democracy" in the region. While US politicians like to repeat this mantra, mostly for the benefit of their domestic constituencies, the United States' decades-long singular public focus on this issue has only served to encourage the Al Saud to waste political capital creating façades of public political participation, such as a consultative council and municipal councils—advisory bodies with no legislative power that face constraints in what they are allowed to discuss. Such cosmetic gestures, if anything, only serve to alienate the growing pool of frustrated and resentful non-royal Saudi intellectual elites. While the United States still retains the influence needed to prod the Al Saud toward reform—and assuming that it still has the will to do so—the lack of adequate scholarship on the politics of the Saudi state renders US leaders bereft of sufficient knowledge, understanding, and the imagination needed to approach this delicate task with any confidence.

The dearth of knowledge on, and limited understanding of, Saudi politics is due to the fact that research on this subject is crippled by a total absence of primary Saudi source material. Unfettered access to government archives, to the extent that they exist at all in any organized form, is forbidden to independent researchers. This deprives Saudi political history of its main source of original information and makes any substantive analysis of the inner workings of the Saudi government virtually impossible. Consequently, like Kremlin-watchers of old, Saudi-watchers today are often reduced to waiting for smoke signals to emerge from the palaces of Riyadh.

Furthermore, the kingdom has always been an inhospitable place for foreign analysts. The country is difficult to access and its society hard to penetrate, even for resident diplomats, who end up spending the majority of their time with fellow expatriates and a tiny pool of westernized Saudis. A public, political, or even social space that is open to interested foreigners and that can be accessed to gauge public opinion has only recently emerged with social media.

This problem is compounded by the absence of frank and honest memoirs written by former members of the Saudi government. The Al Saud have always frowned upon such work; hence, tragically, critical Saudi Arabian political history dies with its participants. This not only prevents outsiders from getting a thorough understanding of Saudi Arabian political history, but also even deprives newer-generation Saudi leaders of this privilege.

Former Oil Minister Ahmad Zaki Yamani was the senior Saudi official who came closest to shining a light on the inner workings of Saudi power by cooperating on a biography written about him in 1989,[1] which was very critical of King Fahd. In the book, Yamani was seen as trying to settle a personal score with the king after having been unceremoniously dismissed by him. It upset Saudi leaders so much that they completely ostracized Yamani and continue to do so to this day. My late father,[2] who worked closely with Saudi leaders for a period of over fifty years, always ignored my pleadings that he write his memoirs, justifying his refusal by saying that he didn't want to break this unwritten rule of discretion.

---

[1] Jeffrey Robinson, *Yamani: The Inside Story* (New York: Atlantic Monthly Press, 1989).

[2] Samir Shihabi. He was successively the Saudi ambassador to Turkey (1964–73); acting deputy foreign minister (1975–77); ambassador to Pakistan (1978–83); and permanent representative to the United Nations (1983–91). In 1991, he was elected president of the General Assembly of the United Nations. His final post (1994–2000) was as ambassador to Switzerland. See http://en.wikipedia.org/wiki/Samir_Shihabi.

The Al Saud never understood or appreciated that if any history about them was to be seen as credible, then it needed to include the good and the bad—and that if the good, on balance, exceeded the bad, then the historical record would ultimately be judged favorably. In any historical work that the government would allow or cooperate with, Saudi leaders had to be presented as nearly perfect human beings who were adored and respected by all—leaders who exhibited almost superhuman skills when dealing with the issues of the day. This is why, for example, a credible history of the founder of the modern dynasty, King Abdul-Aziz, has never been written by a respected international scholar, even though he was a giant of early twentieth-century Arabian history.[3] Unlike another giant of the era, Turkey's Kemal Atatürk, who was widely studied and consequently lionized by history and whose many biographies highlight the good and the bad, history has virtually ignored King Abdul-Aziz.[4]

---

[3] For example, the recent biography of Abdul-Aziz by Michael Darlow and Barbara Bray, proceeding from the admission that the "details of many of the key events in the life of Ibn Saud are still disputed," breaks little new ground. See Michael Darlow and Barbara Bray, *Ibn Saud: The Desert Warrior Who Created the Kingdom of Saudi Arabia* (London: Quartet Books, 2010).

[4] Two notable biographies are Joseph A. Kechichian, *Faysal: Saudi Arabia's King for All Seasons* (Gainesville: University Press of Florida, 2008), and Alexei Vassiliev, *King Faisal of Saudi Arabia: Personality, Faith and Times* (London: Saqi, 2012). Kechichian's book has been described as unbalanced and "excessive in its praise of Faysal"; see Richard L. Russell, "Faysal: Saudi Arabia's King for All Seasons," *Middle East Policy* 16, no. 2 (2009). Vassiliev's book, while a more significant scholarly effort, largely eschews discussing Faisal's domestic policy.

Independent analysts additionally face Saudi Arabia's very effective policy of severely limiting outside analysts' access to the country itself, so preserving this difficult and rare access becomes the lifeblood of "Saudi experts." They have to be extremely careful about what they write and say, so as not to offend their hosts and lose that access, particularly since they very well realize that Saudi rulers, unlike Western politicians, have never had to accept or deal with a hostile domestic media and, therefore, have never developed a tolerance for "bad press."

Such a dearth of original source material for the analysis of Saudi internal politics may be difficult for outside observers to fully appreciate, given the deluge of publicly available information on such matters in Western democracies. For researchers of contemporary American politics, for example, the amount of such material is enormous. Even with history that is still in process, such as with the current Obama administration, which at time of this writing has two years yet remaining in its tenure, credible and critical memoirs and books that include information from key players have already been published. These texts discuss the administration's deliberations and disagreements and the thinking of the president and his key advisors. When you add to that the oceans of historical information about US politics going back for decades, including original documents from presidential libraries, tape recordings like those utilized by Presidents Nixon and Johnson, the constant stream of leaks to the media, ongoing disclosures to Congress, information made available to the media in the course of the US government's daily functioning, information that inevitably emerges in adversarial political campaigns and debates, etc., you have an enormous amount of data about the functioning of the American political system from which to draw intelligent conclusions. An independent analyst of internal Saudi politics simply has *none of the above* at his disposal. He can only judge the output of Saudi politics (i.e., the public actions and decisions made by Saudi leaders), sometimes add to that secondhand information that may be available from foreign sources, and then try to opine on Saudi policy. It is a process that, in comparison to that in the United States, is akin to flying blind.

This lack of adequate scholarship on Saudi politics will continue, despite the very recent advent of social media, which in itself—and in the absence of the other factors explained above—can never provide analysts with anything near a complete picture.

All of this only contributes to many outside stakeholders', and even local elites', false sense of security about the ongoing stability of the Saudi state, while the emerging local and regional enemies of the kingdom—the Sunni Islamists from within and the expansionist jihadis from without, plus the Iranian theocracy and its Arab Shia allies—circle like hungry predators, eagerly waiting for an opportunity to pounce.

Saudi Arabia as a coherent state will, in all likelihood, not be able to survive a fall of the House of Saud. The lack of any other institution of governance with the ability to hold the country together virtually ensures that the removal of Al Saud will bring about a complete breakdown of law and order, the disintegration of the country, and the likely destruction of its oil infrastructure. The geopolitical ramifications of such a collapse will inevitably stretch far beyond the borders of the country. The Saudi kingdom is probably the last major foundational pillar holding up the shaky edifice of the modern Arab nation-state system. Its collapse will not only bring down the remaining states of the Arabian Peninsula and possibly the Levant but may also have a disastrous impact on Egypt's precarious stability.

The failure of many analysts to imagine such potentially apocalyptic outcomes has a lot to do with the fact that the many previous crises in the Arabian Peninsula/Persian Gulf—namely, the decade-long Iraq–Iran war, two US-led wars in Iraq, and the revolutions of the Arab Spring—all happened without causing cataclysmic regional oil production or supply disruptions. This has lulled global oil, commodities, and financial markets into complacency, as reflected in the low geopolitical risk premiums attached to such risks in these markets today.[5]

This complacency is reinforced by the Saudi government's decades-long track record of overcoming the multiple

---

[5] Rob Wile, "Geopolitical Oil Supply Risk Is All But Gone," *Business Insider* (August 15, 2014), accessed August 23, 2014, http://www.businessinsider.com/geopolitical-oil-supply-risk-fades-2014-8.

challenges that have been constantly thrown at it and by people's natural tendency to expect the future to be a linear extrapolation of the present. The continuation of the status quo in Arabia, however, is becoming increasingly unlikely, as the tempo of what French historian Daniel Halévy termed the "acceleration of history" only increases with the explosion of new media and with the spreading democratization of violence.

The emergence of powerful non-state actors across the Arabian Peninsula, Iraq, and the Levant, and their ongoing successes in attacking status quo powers, has captured the imagination of the disgruntled and frustrated youth bulge of this region. Arab masses are beginning to realize that the era of omnipotence of the Arab state is clearly over. Non-state actors like Hezbollah, Hamas, the "Islamic State" (ISIS), al-Qaeda, and others have not only exhibited a capacity to acquire and deploy armaments effectively but, more important, have also succeeded in training and motivating their operatives to reach standards of performance in combat that are proving to be far superior to those of conventional Arab military forces. The intense revolutionary zeal that jihadist fighters are bringing to battle is being met by government troops that exhibit little such enthusiasm. These troops show a lack of willingness to risk their lives for the sake of a ruling order in which they have no particular stake. It is also unlikely, if the jihadi virus continues to spread, that this lack of enthusiasm can be successfully overcome with the involvement of US airpower and intelligence support alone. *For a ruling order to survive, its foot soldiers must want to defend it.*

Saudi leaders have yet to comprehend these tectonic shifts taking place around them.

CHAPTER 2

The Saudi Track Record

Blinded by an aversion to an absolute monarchy that restricts its people's freedoms, deprives its women of equality, and upholds a reactionary Wahhabi interpretation of Islam, the many critics of the House of Saud fail to acknowledge its considerable achievements.

An objective assessment of the performance of the Al Saud as rulers requires context. This should include an appreciation of the limited number of building blocks available to them in building the modern Saudi state, starting with the conditions prevalent in Arabia at the time of the birth of the Saudi kingdom in 1932 and including the environment the kingdom has had to grapple with since then. The assessment also needs to benchmark Saudi performance against other regimes that entered the modern era as independent states from a similar developmental base and then passed through social, economic, and political circumstances and challenges similar to those the kingdom faced. Essentially, a balanced judgment can only be one that is peer-to-peer, not one that compares Al Saud to leaders of developed Western countries or even Muslim countries like Turkey, which began its life as an independent state with a far more developed human endowment and a richer political heritage. Such a peer group should encompass the relatively large oil-rich Arab states like Algeria, Libya, and Iraq, which faced historical circumstances and challenges that were somewhat similar to those encountered by the modern Saudi state.[1]

The Kingdom of Saudi Arabia grew out of the desert region of Najd, central Arabia, which was one of the most underdeveloped spots on earth at the turn of the twentieth century. It had limited human resources and no state infrastructure of any type. While the nascent Saudi state subsequently inherited a tiny Ottoman bureaucracy and a handful of bureaucrats when it occupied the Hejaz in 1925, even here this was governance in its most basic and rudimentary form. The Ottomans, who had ruled the Hejaz prior to its conquest by the Al Saud, had hardly invested in any development, focusing principally on ensuring the physical safety of pilgrims to the holy cities of Mecca and Medina—a critically important point of prestige for Ottoman sultans claiming the Caliphate of Islam. Beyond that, very little had been done; hence, little remained for the Saudi state to inherit.

In comparison, virtually all other Arab states had, at the time of their independence, been colonized directly or indirectly by Western powers for decades. This had left them with at least a rudimentary infrastructure of government: a police force, a bureaucracy, basic laws, and the beginnings of education, health care, etc. The colonial powers, princi-

---

[1]   This comparison should not include the Gulf Arab city-states, given their tiny populations and relatively much larger wealth.

pally Great Britain and France, had, to varying degrees, put these infrastructures in place in these countries. Saudi Arabia, however, having never been colonized, had nothing in terms of an inherited infrastructure of governance on which to build.

The Al Saud took an Arabian Peninsula that lacked all of the above and were still able to put "governance" in place with the very limited financial and human resources at their disposal. First and most important, they imposed law and order where none existed before—on a territory the size of Europe. Then, slowly, as oil money came in, they began to build the country's human and physical infrastructure while securing for their people an uninterrupted period of political stability of over seventy-five years, no mean feat in this most unstable corner of the world. In a country more than three and a half times the size of France, roads, airports, ports, utilities, schools, hospitals, etc., were all put in place to varying degrees. While all this was undoubtedly carried out, as critics correctly point out, in an environment of waste, inefficiency, and corruption, the Saudi state, unlike its peers, was, at least, able to make these basic services available to the majority of its people, in one form or another. At the end of the day, comparatively more value was delivered to the Saudi citizen after decades of oil wealth than to the citizen of virtually any other oil-rich state of a similar size.[2]

---

[2] This subjective conclusion is based on many intangible factors, so it is difficult to quantify in a scientific fashion. I explain my thinking later in the chapter.

One only need look at the disappointing outcome of decades of development in Algeria, Iraq, and Libya to appreciate the logic of this argument. The citizens of those countries today have little of tangible value to show for their decades of oil wealth, despite the fact that Iraq, for example, started from a much higher base of physical and human development than the kingdom did. Algeria, another vivid example, was literally a legal province of France for decades and consequently inherited, upon independence in 1962, the developed physical and governance infrastructure built by the French, plus a sizable French-educated local elite. On top of that, commercial quantities of oil and gas had just been discovered in the country. Despite this valuable "inheritance," the Algerians, after years of suffering the results of incompetent governance and bloody civil war, have consistently lined up in large numbers to immigrate to Europe. Saudis, in comparison, who have traditionally had easier access to travel abroad than any other Middle Eastern peoples, have shown no measurable interest in emigrating from their country. Benchmarks such as these, not absolute criteria that ignore context and circumstance, need to be used when evaluating the performance of the Al Saud as rulers.

The Al Saud historically avoided the pitfalls of political overreach into which so many of their peers stumbled and which brought about considerable destruction of human and physical capital in Saudi Arabia's peer countries. Those countries' rulers, drunk on oil wealth and power, could rarely resist the temptation to overreach, a dangerous habit that inevitably caused them to collide with external powers. In Iraq, Saddam Hussein's folly in attacking Iran and, later, in occupying Kuwait—and his attempts to challenge the United States—destroyed not only him personally but also his country, turning what should have been a wealthy and prosperous nation into a failed state. In Libya, Gaddafi's oil wealth fueled his ambition to play an outsized regional political role. Libya's numerous failed adventures in Africa and the Arab world and its ongoing clashes with the United States and Europe all led to a similarly disastrous outcome for its people. Today, Libya has very little to show for its decades of oil wealth and is now a failed and fragmented state. Iran, whose ambitious revolutionary theocrats spent their oil wealth projecting power across the region, has forced its citizens to pay the painful price of a ten-year war with Iraq and thirty years of debilitating economic sanctions.

The Al Saud, however, with the possible exception of their recent intervention in support of rebels in Syria, generally avoided such overreach. Early on, they developed a realistic and balanced appreciation of their "size" and place in the world. They understood their limitations and never overplayed their hand by trying to behave as a power they were not. Given their oil wealth combined with the country's unique status within Islam, Saudi "power" would have been an intoxicant to a Saudi Gaddafi, Saddam, or Khomeini. Saudi leaders of that ilk would surely have brought ruin upon themselves and their people. The Al Saud also played their cards well by constantly allying themselves with the winners in the global political game, first Great Britain and then the United States after World War II. To understand the implications of Al Saud's keen ability for reading the international balance of power, a skill they have maintained until today, one only has to look at the example of the Ottoman Empire, which aligned with Germany during WWI and was consequently destroyed, or at Reza Shah of Iran,[3] who did the same in WWII and was consequently overthrown and exiled by the Allies.

Al Saud's political wisdom also comes across in the way King Faisal handled the contentious issue in Arab politics of oil as a "weapon." Throughout the 1950s and 1960s, President Nasser of Egypt and other similarly inclined Arab "revolutionary" leaders heaped scorn on the Saudi monarchy for its failure to use the oil weapon against the West, particularly against the United States in response to its constant support of Israel. The full force of Egypt's propaganda machine, driven by its powerful radio channel Sawt al-Arab ("Voice of the Arabs"), focused on the Saudi monarchy, continuously calling it a stooge of America and a traitor to the Arab cause. Saudi rulers, however, understood that playing with oil was a very dangerous game. Aside from knowing that oil was the lifeblood of their economy, they were supplying a crucial commodity that the United States and other Western nations required, and they clearly sensed that the United States would hardly

---

[3]   The first ruler of the Pahlavi dynasty who was exiled to South Africa.

allow a weak but oil-rich country like Saudi Arabia to strangle it economically with its oil. While King Faisal, in a calculated attempt to influence US policy in the Middle East, finally unleashed this weapon in 1973 after the Arab–Israeli War, he made sure not to keep the oil embargo long enough to provoke a US military response. His wisdom in not crossing the United States becomes clear in the records of deliberations that took place in Washington at that time, wherein military action to end the embargo was seriously discussed. At the end of the day, Saudi Arabia was a militarily weak country that could hardly stand up to the might of the United States. The country had the good fortune to be sitting on a quarter of the world's reserves of oil but correctly realized how precarious and vulnerable that position could be. Saudi rulers understood that their country would only be allowed to enjoy the fruits of this bounty if they played their political cards right and avoided antagonizing the United States and the rest of the West. That was a game that very few, if any, of Saudi Arabia's peer countries had the wisdom to appreciate.

Andrew Scott Cooper in his 2011 book *The Oil Kings* highlights Saudi Arabia's vulnerability. Cooper was able to access a large trove of hitherto unpublished records from the Nixon and Ford administrations. These records not only show how close the United States was to taking military action against Saudi Arabia, but they also, interestingly, expose the machinations of the shah of Iran in marketing himself to the Americans as a more "reliable" custodian of Arab oil than the Saudis. The shah and his ambassador, Ardeshir Zahedi, had ongoing discussions over a period of five years with Presidents Nixon and Ford, Secretary of State Henry Kissinger, and other key officials about *occupying Kuwait and Saudi Arabia to "secure" their oil for the West.* These discussions, which began soon after Nixon came to power in 1969, took place in the context of what has been called the Nixon Doctrine (of developing allied regional military powers, in lieu of an exhausted post–Vietnam War United States, to maintain global security). This doctrine fit in very conveniently with the shah's own ambitions to dominate the Persian Gulf and exercise some form of control over Arab oil. Discussions of this nature continued well into the Ford administration, as can be seen in the minutes of a briefing given by Kissinger to President Ford just moments before the shah of Iran was to join them on May 15, 1975, at a White House meeting:

> Kissinger also used these few minutes to inform Ford about US Iranian *contingency planning* [author's emphasis] in the Gulf. Contingency planning had not appeared in Kissinger's briefing paper because it was a secret oral agreement. Now Kissinger told him about it … "Ask him [the shah] about the Middle East," said Kissinger. "He is worried about Saudi Arabia. We told him we would support a paratroop operation [led by Iran] in Saudi Arabia in a crisis. You [Ford] could say that you are aware of this contingency planning."[4]

---

[4]   Andrew Scott Cooper, *The Oil Kings* (New York: Simon and Schuster, 2011), 253.

Cooper's book goes on to quote an article published on July 31, 1975, soon after that meeting, by the syndicated columnist Jack Anderson. Anderson described these policy makers' discussions about Iranian ambitions in Arabia.

According to the latest confidential estimates, however, the Shah's oil reserves will last, at best, for another two decades. This will leave the unpredictable, ambitious, recklessly greedy Shah with little more than a down payment on his glory. Rather than abandon his dream, they [US officials] fear privately, he may march his American-made army into neighboring Saudi Arabia and Kuwait and annex their oil fields.[5]

A weak country that sits on an immensely valuable natural resource is always at risk. Saudi leaders understood this. If they failed to cooperate with the United States and accommodate its requirements, then others, like the imperially inclined Iranians, would eagerly jump up to the plate and offer to "manage" Saudi oil on behalf of the United States. This fundamental vulnerability existed then and *still exists today*. Saudi Arabia's success in retaining full ownership and control of its oil in this politically tricky environment, despite the tremendous pressures it faced in an Arab world that, for decades, had been hostile to America because of its support for Israel, should be recognized and appreciated, particularly by the Saudi people, as a substantial achievement.

---

5   Ibid., 273.

Another point of credit in the Saudi ledger is Al Saud's actual physical management of the country's oil windfall since the resource was discovered in 1938. King Abdul-Aziz invited US oil companies in as investors and operators and encouraged them to build a world-class oil-industry infrastructure. The kingdom then took full ownership of the national oil company, Aramco, in 1980, after negotiating a consensual agreement with its US shareholders. This approach was unlike that of most of the kingdom's peers, who were taken in by the fashionable and populist wave that swept the developing world during that period: nationalizing foreign-owned and foreign-operated oil companies. Mexico, Venezuela, Iraq, Iran, and others consequently alienated the global oil industry and deprived themselves of markets, knowhow, and technology for decades. Even today, many of them are still unable to maximize the returns they should be getting from their oil assets. Mexico, for example, which has mismanaged its oil industry for decades, has only recently begun to allow foreign investment into that sector.

Here, the example of Iran is particularly telling. Iran shares with Qatar ownership of an enormous gas field called the North Dome Field (Iranians know it as South Pars) in the middle of the Persian Gulf. While Qatar, like Saudi Arabia, encouraged foreign investment and kept itself fully plugged into the global industry and has consequently been able to generate enormous returns on its share of the gas field, the Iranians have been unable to participate because sanctions have deprived them of the required technology and support to do so. Consequently, they can only look on bitterly as the Qataris continue to drain the jointly owned field of billions of dollars in gas. Even Iraq, having regained its access to technology and support after the US invasion in 2003, still has a considerable distance to go before it can fully exploit its oil, since the task of rebuilding an antiquated oil industry can take a decade or more.

So many countries' basic mismanagement of the politics and economics of oil deprived those countries' economies and people of hundreds of billions of dollars in oil revenue. Saudi citizens today, by comparison, are in the privileged position of having benefited, albeit perhaps not fully, from political and economic policies that maximized the value of the country's oil assets from the day oil was discovered until today.

In the same vein, the kingdom was an early entrant into the foreign direct-investment space long before encouraging foreign inward investment became fashionable in the developing world. With the establishment of a branch of the Dutch Trading Society (which eventually became ABN AMRO Bank) in Jeddah, Saudi Arabia allowed foreign banks to set up operations on its soil as early as 1926 and also permitted them to operate independently until the late 1970s. Here, again, the government avoided nationalizing these foreign banks and, instead, came up with a midway solution that required them to convert to Saudi public joint-stock companies while retaining a 40 percent ownership stake as well as the right to continue managing the banks. This formula, enormously successful for all parties, allowed the Saudi public to participate in ownership and board supervision of these banks while the foreign partner retained a material equity interest and role. This action raised fresh Saudi capital for these foreign banks, enabling them to expand their operations across the country and quickly grow in size and capability. This allowed all shareholders, domestic and foreign, to earn a great deal of money together while building these banks into major national economic institutions, ones that had a permanent commitment to the country and its people. The joint ventures were so successful that the Citibank joint venture, Saudi American Bank, in the early 1990s had a market capitalization on the Saudi stock exchange that, for a while, was *higher* than its parent's, Citibank, N.A., on the New York Stock Exchange. By avoiding the then-fashionable policy of nationalizing foreign assets and expelling foreign investors, the kingdom's policy makers retained foreign investors and created a consensual formula so they could continue making money in the Saudi market, which also created long-term value for the Saudi economy. In this way, Saudi Arabia developed a banking sector that has consistently been the most advanced and most successful in the whole Middle Eastern region.[6]

---

[6]   I base this subjective conclusion on my experience as chairman of the Board Management Committee of Saudi Hollandi Bank for a period of over ten years, and also on my experience as the founder of the Rasmala Private Equity Fund, which was focused on investing in the financial services sector in the Middle East. In this context, I analyzed and/or invested in banks in the GCC, Egypt, Lebanon, and Jordan.

A similar policy was pursued in the petrochemical industry, where specialized foreign investors were encouraged to set up Saudi industrial operations in the form of joint ventures with SABIC,[7] a holding company established by the government for this purpose, and benefit from the cheap petrochemical feedstock made available to them. The kingdom avoided the common impulse of the time of trying to go it alone and simply purchasing the technology, since it realized that this type of joint venture with global partners would also plug the Saudi petrochemical industry into the global distribution system for marketing and selling its output. This policy encouraged virtually all of the big global players in this sector, like Shell, Exxon, the large Japanese chemical operators, and others, to come into the Saudi market. Today, the kingdom has one of the largest and most profitable petrochemical sectors in the world. Again, none of the kingdom's competitors—Iraq, Iran, Libya, or even the Latin American producers—pursued a similar approach, and none of them even come close to Saudi Arabia today in this space.

Here, one can also look at the miserable track record of resource wealth management that virtually every sub-Saharan African country, post-independence until today,

---

[7] The Saudi Basic Industries Corporation (SABIC), established in 1976, is the publicly held holding company that owns the Saudi share of the joint ventures established with global players in the petrochemical industry. In 2014, SABIC was listed as the world's ninety-fourth largest corporation on the Forbes Global 2000 list, with sales revenues of $50.4 billion, profits of $6.6 billion, and assets standing at $90.2 billion.

has exhibited. While a few of these countries had oil, virtually all of them were endowed with considerable mineral wealth, such as gold, diamonds, copper, bauxite, and high-quality wood forests. Without exception, their management (or, more correctly, mismanagement) of these resources has been such that their countries have little to show for the decades of extracted wealth except for environmental damage, forced displacement of indigenous peoples from their habitats, and civil wars. Furthermore, hardly any of these countries have been able to develop national companies of the quality and capability necessary to run any of their mineral extraction sectors effectively, like a Saudi Aramco or a SABIC, which are managed and staffed today, nearly totally, by Saudi professional and technical personnel. Even in recent years, as Africa became a darling of the foreign investment community, it has not been able to manage its mineral wealth effectively. Howard French in his book *China's Second Continent*[8] talks at length about widespread African public concern regarding China's having been able to secure unjustifiably favorable terms for resource extraction from African governments and its ability to do this without even making any effort to train or transfer knowledge to the local population. The fact that Africa is still unable to take effective control of its extractive industries and sort out these basic and fundamental issues, decades after Saudi Arabia did so very successfully, only reflects well on the Saudi experience.

---

[8] Howard French, *China's Second Continent: How a Million Migrants Are Building a New Empire in Africa* (New York: Knopf, 2014).

All this said, the kingdom was still clearly unable to avoid what historians have come to describe as the "oil (or resource) curse." Oil wealth allowed the government to build a massive top-heavy bureaucracy and to dominate the commanding heights of the country's economy. This created an economy that, today, is nearly totally reliant on government spending and that hardly fosters entrepreneurship or job creation. This, in turn, bred an environment of crony capitalism that inhibited initiative, creativity, and meritocracy. Alongside this, Saudi labor development was ultimately crippled by an education system that was heavily weighted, under Wahhabi pressure, to religious studies and rote memorization, with virtually no critical thinking allowed or encouraged, even at the university level. The net result of all this is a private sector dominated by over 90 percent foreign labor, an underemployed or unemployed and bored crop of Saudi young people who, unlike foreign laborers, refuse menial or low-status work, and a bloated government sector that is constantly being augmented to absorb surplus unproductive Saudi labor.

At the same time, the private sector (neither owned nor controlled by the government) is itself dominated by a few traditional merchant families that were allowed to retain exclusive import agencies for decades. This, for a country like the kingdom that imports virtually everything it requires, means that those lucky families whose fathers or grandfathers were smart enough to secure exclusive import agencies, many more than fifty years ago, can still live off that inheritance today without making any major additional effort. With the advent of the kingdom's accession to the World Trade Organization (2005), these legal monopolies technically ended, but by then the established agents had built up such a scale and presence in the market that competition against them was very difficult, particularly for start-up entrepreneurs. These de facto monopolies obviously feed inflation by depriving the consumer of the benefits of active competition among importers. They also limit entrepreneurial opportunities for young Saudis since the economic space is already filled up with either these traditional merchant families or well-connected parties that can preferentially access the lucrative government-contract pipeline. A cursory look today at the top companies in the Saudi economy will show that, with a few exceptions, these companies were already the dominant players in the economy decades ago. This is in stark contrast to, for example, the top US companies today. While many of today's top US companies, such as Google and Facebook, did not even exist twenty or thirty years ago, most of today's top players in the Saudi economy have been dominant for decades. This encapsulates the difference between the statist Saudi economy, with its many attributes of crony capitalism, and an entrepreneurial, dynamic, meritocratic, and competitive economy like the United States.

In the final analysis, the most important achievement, by far, that kept the country afloat and prosperous, despite the many mistakes made, was Al Saud's preservation and successful political and physical management of the country's oil wealth. This achievement towers over everything else because the Al Saud's peers, without exception, mismanaged their oil inheritance in one way or another.

This success allowed the Al Saud to maintain their top-heavy welfare state, make enormous expenditures with associated waste and corruption, avoid incurring any foreign debt, and still amass large financial reserves of nearly $800 billion by 2014. Adding to that wealth, the state owns very valuable assets such as the national oil company, Aramco, which is the largest oil company in the world today and now belongs entirely to the state. It also owns substantial equity stakes in a large number of other large domestic economic entities, from banks to petro-chemical and industrial concerns. Should it ever need to generate extra revenue in the future, it can easily privatize this large pool of high-quality assets. Of course, the high oil prices of recent years have had everything to do with Saudi Arabia's vast wealth, but as the kingdom looks over its shoulder at its peers in the region and beyond, it can justifiably claim the mantle of having been the most successful among them, by far, in taking advantage of a hydrocarbon-based inheritance.

What the Saudi people did not obtain, obviously, were the political freedoms that a Western citizen takes for granted. Plus, they had to suffer under what a Westerner would consider to be an oppressive socio-religious order that, in particular, gave women even fewer rights than men. On balance, however, and again in comparison to their peers, the Saudi people have come out ahead. This point was driven home to me after Gaddafi's downfall when I spoke with a Libyan friend.[9] "What do the people want?" I asked. "Freedom and democracy?"

"Not really," he answered. "They just want to be like the Khaleejis," i.e., the citizens of the GCC[10] countries who, despite their autocracies, have gotten a much better deal from their rulers than any Libyan, Iraqi, Algerian, or Iranian citizen has ever gotten.

The bottom line is that since its founding in 1932, the Saudi state, in terms of *net tangible value* delivered to its citizens, which I define here as the benefits of oil revenue actually received by a citizen (net of waste and corruption) plus the value to a citizen of years of peace and security, has far exceeded its peer group and the vast majority of resource-rich developing countries. Each one of Saudi Arabia's peer countries not only wasted a larger proportion of its oil wealth in incompetence, corruption, and political adventurism, but also exposed its people to the heavy price of conflict, violence, and isolation from international politics.

While the Al Saud delivered these comparative benefits to the Saudi people, it is still true that absolute monarchies, as the late Professor Samuel Huntington of Harvard University pointed out when describing the "king's dilemma," inevitably sow the seeds of their own destruction by

---

[9]   Ahmed Ben Halim, chairman of Libya Holdings Ltd. and son of former Libyan Prime Minister Mustafa Ben Halim.

[10]   GCC: the Gulf Cooperation Council, whose members are Saudi Arabia, Kuwait, Bahrain, Qatar, the United Arab Emirates, and Oman.

providing their people with education and economic prosperity, which ultimately increases people's expectations to a level where they are no longer willing to tolerate absolute rule. Huntington wrote that "the centralization of power in the monarchy was necessary to promote social, cultural, and economic reform," but that centralization ultimately constrains a monarch when his subjects come to demand a greater say in politics. The king becomes "the victim of his own achievements." For Huntington, there are only three ways by which a monarch can try to escape this dilemma. On the extreme ends, he can either effectively abdicate, accepting a symbolic role in a constitutional monarchy, or cling to power forcefully, challenging with all his might "the broadening of political consciousness." Alternatively, he can try to steer a middle course, "combining monarchical power and popular authority in the same political system." The more developed the country, however, the more acute the dilemma becomes—and the more elusive the third, moderate strategy. Huntington was not optimistic about the survival of traditional monarchies like the Al Saud.[11]

While the wise Saudi citizen today still credits the Al Saud for what they have achieved, the percentage of the population old enough to be able to appreciate these historical achievements grows smaller by the day. As those below the age of twenty-nine make up two-thirds of the current population, the pool of grateful Saudis and those with a memory of the pre-oil days are quickly dying off.

---

[11] Samuel Huntington, *Political Order in Changing Societies* (New Haven: Yale University Press, 1968), 177–91.

CHAPTER 3

The House of Saud

The Al Saud, the royal "family"—which, given its considerable size, can be more accurately described as a tribe—is becoming increasingly isolated not only from the masses, but even from its non-royal elites, as its princely members, increasingly consumed by their traditional (extensive) family obligations and practices, end up mixing mostly with each other.

The monarchy is fortified in its insularity by a virtual absence of any political pressure not only from its public and media but also even from non-royal elites such as military, business, and religious leaders. Saudi elites are so beholden to whatever king is in power for their positions, wealth, and status that the possibility that any of them would dare apply any pressure on the leadership is virtually inconceivable. In addition, since the kingdom does not need to attract foreign capital, either as foreign aid or as debt from multilateral institutions such as the World Bank or the IMF, other traditional channels of pressure for reform, which, historically, developing countries have had to take into account, are, in the kingdom's case, nonexistent.

The royal family's comfortable "bubble" is maintained by an army of retainers who compete to constantly reassure their royal masters that "all is well." This inevitably leads Saudi rulers to ignore or disparage any signals that would otherwise alert them to impending dangers, since such signals are inevitably crowded out by the positive feedback they constantly receive. This condition is hardly one unique to the Al Saud. Autocracies throughout history have suffered from this problem, and few of them have been able to overcome it.

History is littered with examples of such royal self-delusion. British-Iranian scholar Zhand Shakibi, in his book *Revolutions and the Collapse of Monarchy*,[1] highlights a key facet of the shah of Iran's behavior which, he believes, contributed greatly to his overthrow: his self-imposed isolation from unpleasant feedback about the state of his monarchy. "Mohammad Reza tended to ignore negative reports or opinions" and disliked receiving them. His bureaucracy got the message and behaved accordingly. The author describes the difficulties that even the shah's famed security service, the SAVAK, had in keeping their boss adequately informed. They learned to focus on threats that the shah himself identified as important, such as the fringe communist Tudeh Party, and to avoid those threats that did not fit in with the shah's self-perception of being loved by the vast majority of his people. Those threats eventually toppled him.

---

[1]   Zhand Shakibi, *Revolutions and the Collapse of Monarchy* (London: I. B. Taurus, 2007), 187–90, 191, 198.

SAVAK found reporting to the shah on societal cleavages and other possible causes of unrest difficult, if not impossible. The shah unwittingly emasculated his intelligence services ... At the same time the shah increasingly did not want to hear criticism and words of disagreement from his ministers.

Even the shah's own wife, Queen Farah, found that she was unable to relay unpleasant political news to him. The author quotes her as saying,

He [the shah] refused to listen ... I saw problems while His Majesty [HM] saw the achievements. In bed we would compare notes. I would report about what was going wrong in the regions I had just toured. HM would try to dismiss my reports as exaggerated or one-sided. ... Sometimes he would get impatient and edgy. "No more bad news please!" HM would command. And I would, naturally, change the subject.

The author concludes, "The shah's growing tendency to ignore advice that contradicted his own views and to brand such views as pessimistic or negative ossified the Pahlavi system. Many in government fell into line and told him what he wanted to hear."

Edmond Taylor in his classic *The Fall of the Dynasties*[2] describes a telling discussion between Nicholas II, the last tsar of Russia, and the British ambassador who desperately wanted to alert the monarch to the dangers he saw

---

[2]   Edmond Taylor, *The Fall of the Dynasties: The Collapse of the Old Order, 1905–1922* (New York: Dorset Press, 1963), 21.

threatening the Russian monarchy. "Your Imperial Majesty may be losing the confidence of your people," the ambassador told Nicholas.

"The more important question, Excellency," the insular tsar responded, "is not whether my people have lost their confidence in me, but whether I have lost confidence in my people." Upon hearing that arrogant and delusional response, the ambassador realized that the monarchy was doomed.

Today, the Saudi monarchy, comfortably ensconced in its positive-feedback loop, remains shielded from harsh realities by a subservient press and even by timid foreign counterparties who continue to humor Saudi leaders in person, although many privately express concern about Al Saud's prospects for survival. Time and again, I have heard US and UK officials and analysts tell me, "They [Al Saud] cannot survive." Yet in meetings with senior members of the Al Saud, even in non-official social settings or in lectures and conferences, these people invariably avoid raising any issues that could potentially unsettle the royal person.

I once attended a meeting in Riyadh of a few US academics with a senior Saudi prince, a highly sophisticated and educated individual. During our discussion, the prince twice made the argument that "the kingdom does not need democracy since we have our majlis system."[3] Not one of

---

[3] Majlis is the traditional practice of an Arabian tribal leader's receiving petitioners. Theoretically, this is open to all, but, as practiced today, it tends to be a cosmetic exercise.

those academics challenged him on that statement. In fact, they gave him every indication that they agreed with everything he said. After we left, the academics commented on the prince's "ridiculous" point about the majlis system, which they considered to be a woefully outdated political mechanism for Arabian rulers to interact with their people. Yet not one of them had even gently disputed that point in the prince's presence. This is hardly a unique or isolated example.

Isolation helps encourage Saudi royals to obsess on intrafamily politics, principally the constant competition among them over the spoils of power. They operate as if these issues, rather than the mounting internal and external threats to their rule, are their paramount concerns. This unhealthy obsession with family politics, at the expense of more critical issues, is largely driven by the Al Saud family's enormous size, which is the fundamental structural problem that plagues them.

The current Saudi royal family structure was created by the founder of the modern Saudi state, King Abdul-Aziz, who fathered nearly ninety children, all of whom were recognized as royal progeny. Such prolific reproduction was, in part, smart politics, since it bound Abdul-Aziz to a number of important families and tribes in Arabia. But it was also the traditional prerogative of a wealthy and powerful Arab sheikh who—given the conventional and austere Islamic environment of central Arabia at the time of Saudi Arabia's establishment—had none of the more modern worldly pleasures available to a king, pleasures that were available, for example, to his royal contemporaries, the kings of Egypt and Iraq. This left him only with the sharia-compliant avenues of marriage or concubinage for his entertainment, a privilege in which he fully indulged. In so doing, he set a precedent for his brothers and cousins to emulate. They, in turn, produced large numbers of progeny, which today translates into thousands of claimants to royal privilege. According to some estimates, there are now over ten thousand holders of princely titles. The exact figure is a tightly held state secret.

The problem of managing royal progeny and claimants to power and privilege is an age-old one that has been addressed throughout history in a variety of ways. The Ottomans, history's longest-surviving dynasty (1299–1922), were particularly adept at, if rather brutal in, addressing this problem. Traditionally, each newly crowned sultan would have all of his brothers immediately strangled. However distasteful this was, it certainly accomplished the task, namely keeping the Ottomans' numbers manageable and allowing them to survive as a ruling dynasty for more than six hundred years. When the Ottomans abandoned the practice of fratricide in the early seventeenth century, they found gentler ways of eliminating potential contenders from within the family.[4] In Christendom, on the other hand, monarchs had to be monogamous. Only their legitimate issue was in line to the

---

[4]   Colin Imber, "The Ottoman Empire (Tenth/Sixteenth Century)," in *The New Cambridge History of Islam*, ed. Maribel Fierro, vol. 2 (Cambridge: Cambridge University Press, 2010), 352.

throne, with the principle of primogenitur[5] strictly established. The many illegitimate progeny of European royalty, if acknowledged, were sometimes awarded noble titles but had no legal claim to power. This kept all of these families at a manageable size.

King Abdul-Aziz established the principle that the throne would pass on to his sons by seniority (i.e., the first son would be first in line, the second son would be second, and so forth) rather than following the principle of primogeniture (where the line would pass from the first son to *his* son), which has been the custom in most ruling families throughout history. With thirty-four sons who survived into adulthood, Saudi Arabia's first king probably found it difficult to disenfranchise thirty-three of them, even though his decision at the time to disenfranchise his many brothers and cousins from a claim to the throne was not one that was easily made. It is still resented by many of their descendants today, given that many of Abdul-Aziz's brothers and cousins had fought with him and played key roles in founding the kingdom. In compensation, he allowed them and their offspring to retain royal titles and access to the full range of financial benefits, privileges, and immunities associated with membership in the ruling family, a practice that remains in place to this day.

In the Al Saud family, each member, of either gender, receives a monthly salary according to rank and seniority—

---

[5]   Primogeniture is the right, by law or custom, of the firstborn male child to inherit the throne, in preference to siblings.

starting at birth. In addition, the state pays their utility bills and awards them cash grants, grants of land, and privileged access to government contracts. This practice, to a lesser degree, is also extended to the Al Sheikh family, who are descendants of the founder of the Wahhabi movement, and to others. This all adds up to tens of thousands of people who receive incomes and extensive privileges from the state for no reason other than birth—a not inconsequential burden on the state treasury, one that only increases with time as these families all, naturally, grow. The exact sum involved in maintaining this system with funds from the public treasury remains a closely guarded state secret.

This practice began in the era of King Abdul-Aziz when oil wealth started to gush in. King Saud, his successor, indulged himself and his sons financially to a level far beyond the state's ability to absorb at that time. He quickly proceeded to bankrupt the country and was eventually removed from power. His successor, King Faisal, implemented a strict policy of financial prudence that involved substantial reductions in royal spending and financial privileges—actions that, while politically sound, were met with the family's resentment. Faisal, however, was a strong ruler who was able to impose his will on them all.

Saudi royals' financial discipline, however, evaporated after Faisal was assassinated in 1975. His successors proceeded to remove from office their tight-fisted uncle Musaid, whom Faisal had made finance minister expressly for that purpose, and then quickly reverted to old habits. This was made all the more possible by the 1973 oil boom, which brought unimaginable wealth surging into the country's coffers. The profligacy was to continue into the next decades, hardly affected by the 1985–2003 recession and drop in oil price. It continues to this day, despite King Abdullah's unsuccessful efforts to moderate royal expenses and privileges early in his reign.

The accumulated cost of supporting this enormous royal family has become a very contentious source of resentment for the Saudi public, as previously confidential details have now begun to leak out on social media. A recent example appeared in July 2014, in the financial statements published by one of the publicly listed electricity companies. Dissidents quickly noted and publicized on Twitter a footnote to these statements, showing that the state treasury settled, in 2013, $700 million in unpaid "VIP" electricity bills with this company alone. Such action, in an environment wherein the average Saudi may have his electricity, water, or phone service cut off for failing to pay a small overdue bill, is, needless to say, highly controversial and unpopular with the public.

In another example, dissidents have exposed some of the royal family's vast land holdings across the country, using Google Earth to identify the many tracts of land gifted to royals by the king. This is a particularly sore point for average Saudis, since many of them cannot find affordable land on which to build a home. Also, large tracts of public land in the countryside, which people used to camp on (a favorite pastime of a people with bedouin roots), are now fenced off by royals and inaccessible to the average citizen.

This issue, which has been hashtagged on twitter as "Shubook" (fences), has become a key rallying cry for government dissidents and critics.

Despite such increasing public awareness of the privileges associated with royal status, the monarchy, instead of working to somehow reduce the "massive footprint" of the royal family, has done the exact opposite by *increasing* the size of the royal family in the last decade. They did this by according princely status to three additional families, distant cousins of theirs—the Muqrin, Farhan, and Thinayan families—officially transforming them from commoners to princes. The misplaced priority driving this decision was the monarchy's desire to assuage the dissatisfaction of these distant cousins, who had always felt that they had unfairly not been classified as princes when the modern state was born, and hence rectify this "mistake." Here, the politically flawed focus on the feelings of Al Saud's probably already somewhat privileged distant cousins rather than on the undoubtedly more important issue of Saudi public opinion is a clear indicator of a royal family disconnected from the public and over-engrossed in its internal affairs. At the end of the day, all such a step did was increase the already massive footprint that the royals have across the "commanding heights" of society. Thus, it serves only to exacerbate the already onerous political burden that thousands of princes and princesses bring upon the state.

All of the above takes place in an environment where the members of the ruling class benefit from de facto legal immunity. Draconian by Western standards, the laws of the Islamic justice system, while strictly applied to the common person, are rarely applied to members of the ruling class. This strikes at the heart of the legitimacy of Islamic rule, given that justice applied uniformly to all is a fundamental pillar of sharia law, which the state claims to uphold. This issue is another point that government critics highlight at every opportunity.

At the same time, some high-profile royals cannot seem to resist the international limelight and unwisely allow the media into their palaces, planes, and yachts to record and publicize their extravagant lifestyles. Government dissidents then pick up, circulate, and comment on these news stories. It is one thing for the common person to hear rumors about royal lifestyles, but to see the evidence on YouTube or Instagram is particularly provocative. Providing such easy ammunition for your enemies to use is particularly unwise, yet these princes continue to do this—and the king seems unable to rein them in.

The government's inability to control this large family is a symptom of a weakening leadership that is unable to bridle its many members as successfully as it did in the past. The problem here is that any member of this vast family, as long as he or she holds the title of Saudi "prince" or "princess," carries a brand risk for the whole royal family and the Saudi state. Any prince's misdeed reflects badly on both. With the increased number of these royals operating all over the country and around the world, this risk is increasing by the day.

By according formal princely status to thousands of people, the monarchy has created a large (and clearly identified by title) privileged and entitled class that takes precedence, in virtually every sphere of life, over all other citizens. This class inevitably competes with and crowds out the large pool of upcoming educated and ambitious Saudi commoners who face limited prospects of advancement and success in such a blatantly unmeritocratic environment. History has taught us that when the nobility starts to crowd out the upcoming bourgeois classes, trouble lies ahead.[6]

Yet the Al Saud's phenomenal success to date has numbed the family to such logic and has increased their self-confidence to a degree that they operate as if the rules of history will never apply to them. By persistently defying their skeptics who, for decades, have forecast the royal family's imminent demise, they have become dulled to the potential consequences of a changing world around them. They

---

[6] Many revolutions in modern history were fueled by popular resentment of the entrenched privileges of the aristocracy. The first was in France in 1789, to be followed by the Mexican, Russian, Cuban, and Iranian Revolutions, among others. While the literature on revolutions tends to focus on a multiplicity of contributing factors, it nevertheless "widely agree[s] upon ... [the] vulnerabilities" of the "repressive, exclusionary, personalist state which ... reposes on the combination of repression of lower-class forces and exclusion of both the growing middle classes and the economic elite from political participation." Such states have been dubbed variously "sultanistic," "neopatrimonial," "personalist authoritarian," and "mafiacratic" (John Foran, *Taking Power: On the Origins of Third World Revolutions* [Cambridge: Cambridge University Press, 2005], 20, 285).

exhibit an understandable but misplaced hubris borne out of decades of beating the odds.

While there are a number of royals who understand these mounting risks, they stay remarkably timid and silent in family councils, despite their realization that perpetuating the status quo puts their futures, and even their lives, at risk. This is a result of the Saudi royals' obsessive respect for age and patriarchy, which is rigorously drilled into them from childhood. It leads them to virtually blindly defer to their elders. This is noticeable even among the "younger" generation of royals who themselves are in their fifties and sixties and hold top positions in government. This practice, combined with the climate of extreme politeness and protocol that pervades intrafamily interactions, means that contentious debate at the top is nonexistent. Government policy ends up being made exclusively by the king and the very few key advisors and relatives he trusts at that moment.

The lack of debate even at the highest levels of government often results in decisions that are not carefully thought through or adequately analyzed. The extremely tight circle of ultimate decision makers at the top means that policy is often made impulsively behind closed doors, with inevitably mixed results.

CHAPTER 4

The Wahhabi Ulema and the Jihadi Threat

The Wahhabi establishment is the organized group of Saudi Sunni ulema (scholars/clergy) who uphold the theological beliefs and opinions of Sheikh Muhammad ibn Abdul-Wahhab, whose alliance in 1744 with the founder of the Al Saud dynasty, Emir Muhammad ibn Saud, succeeded in channeling the immense energy, drive, and passion of that stern religious movement into a force that conquered most of Arabia in the eighteenth century. This alliance has ruled large parts of the Arabian Peninsula, on and off, since that time. It continues to do so today.

In 1902, when King Abdul-Aziz returned from exile in Kuwait, where his family had settled after their defeat and removal from power in 1891, to regain his ancestral domain, there was only one group that could in any sense be called an institution in Najd, central Saudi Arabia—and that was the Wahhabi ulema. They carried out the only public service role that was then available to the people of Najd, which was resolving disputes, providing religious education, and serving as imams of the mosques—a role that effectively made them community leaders.

These Wahhabi ulema immediately recognized an opportunity in supporting Abdul-Aziz as the new ruler, since they recognized in him a strong leader, one who also came from their traditional political ally, the Al Saud, and who would impose much-needed law and order and help them spread their teachings to the rest of the Arabian Peninsula, just as Abdul-Aziz's ancestors had done before him.

The Wahhabis consequently proclaimed their loyalty to Abdul-Aziz, a very important step that gave the young chief immediate legitimacy as the new ruler of Riyadh. They then organized themselves to spread out among the towns and tribes of Najd to lobby the people to support Abdul-Aziz as their new ruler and enlist them in a jihad to conquer the Arabian Peninsula. They argued that in doing so, the people of Najd would be carrying out God's will by spreading Wahhabism and the rule of Al Saud to the many "deviant" rulers, towns, and tribes of Arabia. In this case, anybody who resisted Abdul-Aziz was conveniently classified as a deviant and hence subjected to this hostile jihad.

This "political campaign" undertaken by the Wahhabis on behalf of the Al Saud, a grassroots political endeavor in a very real sense, was very effective due to the perseverance and dedication that these Wahhabi preachers displayed with the townspeople and bedouins of Najd as they lived among them and indoctrinated them with the "duty" to fight for the Al Saud. Prominent clerics spent months or even years with some tribes to ensure their active participation in the conquests of Abdul-Aziz.

This campaign was also successful because these ulema already had a virtual monopoly on the religious space of central Arabia at that time. Wahhabism already had strong roots among the townspeople of Najd, while the bedouins were Muslims in only the most superficial sense, abiding by tribal habits much more strongly than by Islamic tradition. This was an arid soil that the Wahhabis were able to water and, therefrom, grow a "crop" of Muslims who were perfectly suited to their ideological worldview.

They also cleverly allowed the bedouins to mix this "holy" jihad with the traditional bedouin pastime of ghazu, basically the organized raiding and plunder of their enemies. Classifying the enemies of King Abdul-Aziz as "enemies of God" and "deviants" gave the bedouins religious sanction not only to attack them but also to plunder them and walk away with booty. This politically useful formula, hardly the first time such logic was deployed in either Islamic or Christian history, was remarkably successful and allowed Abdul-Aziz to unite and create what is today the Kingdom of Saudi Arabia.

Abdul-Aziz, however, once he achieved his objective of forming the Saudi state, soon faced the problem of restraining the energy and passion the Wahhabis had unleashed among these bedouins. When a large group of bedouin warriors (called the Ikhwan, or brethren) who had fought for Abdul-Aziz revolted against his failure to continue the jihad and allow them to attack targets in the British imperial protectorates of Iraq, Jordan, and the Gulf—all of which presented considerable opportunities for plunder—

the king faced a severe internal political crisis and eventually had to fight the Ikhwan and put them down. Here again, the support of the Wahhabi leadership, which recognized the danger of allowing the energy they had unleashed to continue unchecked, was crucial in giving the newly proclaimed king sanction for this fight. The rebellious Ikhwan were now conveniently reclassified as deviants.

The genius of unleashing Islamic fanaticism to serve the project of Saudi state building and then restraining it when it had outlived its original purpose was something that required the full support and involvement of the Wahhabi leadership. Abdul-Aziz appreciated that these ulema were an integral part of his success and knew that he would need them no less to hold his state together going forward.

A formula built on the historic partnership between Al Saud and the ulema was worked out. The ulema would allow the Al Saud freedom to manage foreign affairs, the economy, security, etc., and the ulema, in turn, would define "Saudi Islam" strictly as Wahhabism; control all religious institutions, including the two holy mosques of Islam in Mecca and Medina, with the associated privileges and stature in the wider world of Islam; supervise education and the social and cultural space; and control and exclusively staff the judicial system.

Dedicated to their mission, the ulema set out to achieve their objectives. Passionate believers in their cause, they projected an image of piety and frugality and hence acquired considerable status among the Saudi people. Unlike the more remote royals, they were in daily contact with the people, interacting with them, guiding them, educating them, and leading them in prayer. Their effectiveness in carrying out their mission bred a Saudi people programmed, to this day, to look to the ulema for answers to virtually all questions of life.

The information monopoly that the Wahhabis put in place was also leveraged to uphold the rule of the Al Saud. No other disruptive ideology was allowed into the Saudi public space, whether it consisted of Western liberal ideas or the Arab nationalism and socialism that swept the region in the fifties and sixties. The Wahhabis drilled into their flock, the Saudi people, the sanctity of obeying their ruler, a member of the House of Saud, under any circumstances, short of his preventing the people from practicing Islam. This concept of ta'at wali al-amr, essentially an unquestioning obedience to rulers, while a widely held Sunni concept, had been taken to an extreme by the ideological godfather of Wahhabism, the medieval Damascene theologian Ibn Taymiyyah, who argued that "one night of disorder is worse than sixty years of unjust rule." Taken by the Wahhabis literally, this logic basically indoctrinated the Saudi public with the religious duty to show unquestioning obedience to the Al Saud under any conceivable circumstance. It also left any checking-and-balancing role on the absolute power of the Al Saud to the ulema elders, who would use their own judgment and deal with the monarch on a strictly private basis. Public dissent, in any form, was classified as "fitna," a legal term in Islam meaning "sedition," and was subject to the most severe sanctions.

The energy, passion, and prestige that the ulema brought to the table, and their authority with the masses, played a major role in maintaining social and political stability during what could easily have been a tumultuous transition from life in a barren desert to life in the twenty-first century. For any society to jump from abject poverty in the isolated deserts of Arabia to vast wealth and contact with the outside world in one generation is disruptive, to say the least. The oppressive hold that this clerical establishment had on society at least held Saudi society together through this time of turbulent change, an important and valuable accomplishment not to be underestimated.

Al Saud nurtured this alliance by allowing the Wahhabis to get a sizable share of the substantial oil-wealth-funded national economic pie. They did this by permitting the Wahhabis to build an enormous patronage network across the country that was funded by the state treasury. An estimate made in 1995[1] placed the number of employees working for institutions that the Wahhabis controlled and, hence, that were subject to their patronage at close to six hundred thousand individuals (Saudis and foreigners).[2]

---

[1] Dr. Anwar Abdallah, *Al-Ulama wal-Arsh* (London: al-Rafid Publishing House, 1995).
[2] Ibid.

That covered, in addition to the classical religious institutions such as mosques, the courts, the notaries public, local and international Islamic associations, the many Islamic universities, colleges, and sharia schools, and so forth. Today, that number is probably even larger.

This formula generally worked smoothly, although the inevitable clash between strict Wahhabi doctrine and the young state's need to adapt to modernity caused ongoing friction between the ulema and the throne. Modern laws and regulations like customs and commercial laws that did not emanate from sharia were introduced by King Abdul-Aziz. The ulema resisted them. The radio, telegraph, and telephone were allowed into the country. The ulema did not understand these technologies and feared that they would be disruptive. King Faisal insisted on the introduction of women's education, an extremely unsettling and alien idea to the ulema at that time. Eventually, the monarchy successfully managed these bumps in the road, although a hard-core element among the Wahhabis that saw all these "modern" steps as sacrilegious remained seething in the background, only to explode onto the surface with the attack on the Grand Mosque of Mecca in 1979 by Juhayman al-Otaibi and his followers. This incident shocked the state. Combined with the additional shock of the "Islamic" Revolution in Iran in that same year, it drove King Fahd to tone down many public manifestations of "modernity" that offended the Wahhabis. He also simultaneously opened the spigots of public funding even wider to these ulema and their pet projects.

Despite the many headaches the ulema caused their monarchs, the wisdom of ensuring that this conservative and reactionary establishment eventually bought into the government's modernization policies can be better appreciated when one looks at the record of other Muslim leaders in the twentieth century who took a much more aggressive approach to modernization and the sidelining of "tradition."

A particularly telling example of a flawed approach can be seen today in Afghanistan's continuingly stubborn social conservatism, particularly regarding the emancipation of women. People today are probably not aware of the story of King Amanullah Khān (1919–29) of Afghanistan. A progressive monarch for his time, he married a Damascus-born woman, Soraya Tarzi, who was well educated and thoroughly westernized by the standards of that time. Under her influence, he imposed a modernist constitution on the country that granted freedoms and equality for all, with a particular focus on women's rights, education, and emancipation. Queen Soraya went so far as to tear off her veil in a *public* ceremony. She appeared in Western dress when traveling all over the country and the world with her husband and was pictured in the media beside him. Such daring reform was celebrated in the West. Both king and queen were awarded honorary doctorates by the University of Oxford. At home, however, these reforms and actions thoroughly incensed the mullahs of what was a very conservative Muslim society. They went all-out against the king and his queen in public protests that nearly led to a civil war. Amanullah finally had to abdicate and leave the country with his wife in 1929. His reforms were subsequently overturned.

In the 1950s and 1960s, Amanullah's successors made further attempts to enact similar reforms, but they were all eventually destined to fail under the determined and passionate resistance of the reactionary mullahs. The Afghanistan of today, with its Taliban-style social model, is, if anything, a clear testament to the folly of trying to push conservative Muslim societies too quickly forward in the face of clerical resistance. That the Al Saud had the patience to drag their clerical establishment along with modernization and not exceed the outer limits of what that establishment would tolerate resulted in, we see now, a much wiser and more permanent path to modernization and societal development, not least because the country also avoided much bloodshed and violence in the process.

Over time, however, the Saudi monarchy became increasingly tired of the ulema's interference and reactionary attitude. As the influential clerics at the apex of the Wahhabi establishment eventually passed away by the late 1990s, Saudi rulers began to replace them with ulema of lesser stature. This was a deliberate strategy, one that sought to reduce Wahhabi influence on the monarchy. It was also an indication of an increasingly confident and secure royal family, one that was becoming less willing to share the stage with the Wahhabi leadership or acknowledge the extent of their historic partnership. This step, while freeing the hand of Saudi rulers to exercise absolute political power, diminished the prestige of the newer crop of government-appointed Wahhabi leaders and scholars. People consequently began to see the new clerical leadership as a weak and subservient partner to the Al Saud, one that did little but rubber-stamp the ruling family's decisions.

This issue first erupted in public with the shock of Saddam Hussein's 1990 invasion of Kuwait. King Fahd's decision to call on the "infidel" United States to liberate Kuwait and deal with Saddam shocked the rank and file of the Wahhabi community. The Wahhabi leadership's subsequent public sanction of the king's decision in a controversial fatwa was extremely unpopular. After all, people had always been taught that an alliance with the "infidel" against fellow Muslims was sacrilege. The theological gymnastics that the Wahhabi elders had to perform to justify their support of King Fahd's decision were hard for the Wahhabi rank and file to swallow and seriously undermined these elders' credibility.

This provoked a major rift in public consensus about the Wahhabi community and led to an unprecedented series of public letters calling for government reform. These letters were addressed to King Fahd and signed by a group of younger, more aggressive Wahhabi scholars (the Sahwa ulema) and activist academics. The most important of these documents was produced in 1992. Called a "Memorandum of Advice" to the ruler, it laid out in considerable detail a series of political demands, including more independence for the clerical establishment and the judiciary, financial transparency in government spending, and other ideas. A public step like this one had never before been taken in the country. It not only was a first in terms of public political demands from within the Wahhabi establishment, but it also signified a revolt within the establishment by the younger scholars against their elders, the latter of whom abhorred insubordination and public dissent. The government responded harshly to this letter and incarcerated most of its signatories.

Released a few years later, some of them, like Salman al-Awdah, Safar al-Hawali, and Muhsin al-Awaji, remained in the kingdom and made peace with the state (while attempting to push the envelope in public debate and discussion, with some success). Others, like Saad al-Faqih and Muhammad al-Massari, went into exile in the United Kingdom and began to actively oppose the Saudi government and call for its overthrow.

The pool of "young Turks" within the wider Wahhabi establishment grew larger and bolder over time and began to question many of (Saudi state) Wahhabism's most important principles: the elders' unquestioned obedience to the Al Saud; the fact that these elders ignored the supposed "un-Islamic" policies of the royal family; and their support of a Saudi foreign policy that was "hostile to Islam."

This insurgency within the scholarly Wahhabi class was supported by the arrival of satellite television broadcast from outside the kingdom in the 1990s, which was followed by the rise of the Internet and, finally, the advent of social media in recent years. This ended the critical monopoly on information that the Wahhabi elders and the government had enjoyed for so long. Today, media platforms that give ambitious and charismatic young Islamist scholars an independent channel to reach the Saudi public, express their views, and build a large following have proliferated. The government has responded with a massive investment in monitoring technology and infrastructure, but, like other governments seeking to control this unruly space, its efforts will inevitably fall short.

These modern political Islamist "entrepreneurs" began using the same Wahhabi ideology that their elders had used so successfully for decades in support of the government. But this time, they *twisted it to their own political purposes* in order to create Islamic justification for disobedience and even, in some cases, violent jihad against the rulers of Arabia. This probably contributed to the emergence of Saudi terrorist cells associated with al-Qaeda soon after 9/11. With a series of bombs placed around the country, al-Qaeda succeeded in killing many innocent civilians, which consequently inflamed Saudi public opinion against the organization. The government was eventually able to fight these terrorists successfully and destroy them. This was achieved by a combination of strong public support and a dramatic improvement in the state's antiterrorist capabilities and security infrastructure.

The fight against these radical militants allowed the government to paint all those who opposed it with the brush of terrorism and consequently to intimidate many of its critics into submission. This approach was quite success-ful in keeping the hostile trend of rebellious activity at bay until the start of the Syrian Civil War in 2011. That crisis, however, in which the government took the active and public position of opposing the Assad regime, allowed many clerics and scholars to reemerge under the cover of supporting the Syrian opposition and thereby gain public prominence. Once out of the box, many of them subse-quently widened their focus and brought their energies back to bear on domestic politics.

These dissident clerics and scholars began focusing on trying to undermine the Saudi people's very successful adoption to date of the concept of ta'at wali al-amr (unques-tioned obedience to the rulers), the doctrinal principle of the Saudi Wahhabi state that is drilled into Saudis from childhood. The enemies of Al Saud realize that this is a critical point that they will have to erode in the minds of the Saudi people if they are ever to get them to rebel against their royal rulers. To this end, dissidents have filled social media with arguments alleging that the Saudi state has forfeited its right to be obeyed by its citizens since it has been, and still is, working "against the interests of Islam." Here, while issues of governance such as autocracy and the lack of adequate Shura (the sharia directive that rulers should consult) are sometimes mentioned, such concepts, being somewhat too highbrow in nature for the masses to absorb, tend to be replaced in the public discourse with more emotive arguments, such as claims that Al Saud "conspire" with the Americans, Israelis, and/or Iranians to kill Muslims in Syria, Iraq, Gaza, Egypt, Yemen, and elsewhere. Like aspiring politicians everywhere, members of the Saudi opposition are as good as the next person at warping and dramatizing complex political issues in their quest to inflame public opinion against the state. Given the overt Saudi support for the Sisi coup in Egypt, Saudi Arabia's ongoing support for the US drone program in Yemen, and, most recently, Saudi participation in the US-led allied attacks on ISIS in Syria and Iraq, among other things— plus the inevitable collateral damage to innocent civilians associated with all these actions—Saudi dissidents have a lot of inflammatory material to use in this regard.

A recent (July 2014) very high-profile example of the attack on the concept of obedience is seen in the comments made by prominent Kuwaiti Wahhabi cleric Hajjaj al-Ajmi, who gained a popular following among Saudi youth as an outspoken supporter and promoter of jihad against the Assad regime in Syria. He was interviewed on a popular Saudi television talk show and proceeded to dispute boldly the Saudi interpretation of ta'at wali al-amr and its applicability to the rulers of Saudi Arabia and the Gulf. He called these rulers illegitimate under Islamic law and unworthy of the people's obedience. Such revolutionary talk on live prime-time television was previously unheard of in the kingdom. It shocked the public and more so, obviously, the authorities. The government immediately expelled the cleric from the kingdom and sanctioned the popular TV host, but the damage was done.

This ideological schism within the Wahhabi clergy, between the older conservative government-appointed clerics who support upholding the established political order and the younger, more charismatic, and politically bold clerics who are gaining a wide following on social media, is obviously very dangerous for Al Saud. It hits at the core of their legitimacy and, in undermining the established elders of the Wahhabi movement, threatens to bring down the foundational basis for their rule.

Yet in fighting this dangerous trend, the Al Saud have not been very creative. With few exceptions, they have fallen back on their traditional formula of total reliance on the Wahhabi elders to control and delegitimize these younger clerics. These senior ulema, however, lack the charisma and public appeal that many of these "young Turks" who are capturing the public imagination have. Hence, this approach does not seem very likely to succeed. As a result, the major pillar of the rule of the House of Saud, the Wahhabi pillar upholding the principle of unquestioned obedience to the country's rulers in the name of Islam, is now being very dangerously shaken.

Today, evidence available from social media[3] shows that militant Islamist jihadi movements retain considerable public support inside the kingdom. Since this support covers many causes, some publicly considered legitimate

---

[3]   Rachel Levy, "Could Saudi Arabia Be the Next ISIS Conquest?" *Vocativ* (June 23, 2014), accessed July 31, 2014, http://www.vocativ .com/world/iraq-world/saudi-arabia-next-isis-conquest/.

by the government (such as the battle against the Syrian regime and the Palestinian fight against the Israelis), and others criminalized by the government (such as support for al-Qaeda, the Muslim Brotherhood, the Islamic State, and others), it is difficult to identify the hard-core anti-Saudi-government component within these movements. Also, the government's near total success in stamping out jihadi terrorism in the country over the last decade has either pushed these groups deep underground to wait for the right opportunity to emerge or forced them to flee the country.

Getting an accurate handle on the size and strength of the domestic Saudi jihadi community is therefore difficult,[4] but Saudi participation in jihadi activity in Yemen, Iraq, and Syria—and the support that jihadis get on social media from within the kingdom—allows the argument that these groups constitute a serious threat to the country and its rulers. Any upcoming trigger/crisis that affects the public's perception of state power may allow these jihadis to make a move. The presence of the Islamic State on the kingdom's northern borders and the presence of al-Qaeda in the

---

[4] The Washington Institute, on October 14, 2014, published an article based on polls taken in the kingdom that showed that ISIS had "almost no popular support" in Saudi Arabia. Such polls in a country that has no experience with independent public polling, in which Saudis would be asked if they supported a terrorist organization, cannot be considered credible. A Saudi polled today can never be sure that his opinion will not reach the authorities in some form and subject him to sanction, so he will most likely provide "safe" answers.

Arabian Peninsula on its southern borders, and the likely presence of these groups' followers and sympathizers inside the country, many of them armed and experienced in insurgency, indicates that a jihadi attempt to overthrow the state is increasingly likely. To this end, like all aspiring revolutionaries throughout history, these revolutionaries are working hard to ignite the fires of class conflict in the country. Additionally, given that the traditional Wahhabi religious establishment has very little to say about economic inequality, the more radical Islamists are able to monopolize the call for social justice.

History has taught us that it is not absolute but relative levels of wealth and prosperity that drive class conflict. Today, the have-nots in Arabia—essentially, those who perceive themselves as having not gotten their "fair" share of Saudi Arabia's oil wealth and who, in a previous era, would have looked to raise the flag of socialism, Arab nationalism, or Baathism to attack the status quo—eagerly adopt the mantle of militant Islamism as the *ideology du jour*, since they perceive it as the weapon most likely to succeed in tearing down the high walls of royal power, wealth, and privilege in Arabia.

These days, international observers are focusing intently on radical Islam (Islamism/jihadism) and its attributes, debating how its extremist messages can be fought "in the realm of ideas." Here, they may be failing to consider that, in most cases, radical Islam may simply be the contemporary *flag of convenience* for the rebels who are determined to overturn the present ruling order in the region. Like many of the revolutionary ideologies that swept the world and the region in decades past, Islamism may simply be the ideology that rebels have recognized as the most potent tool to leverage in achieving their revolutionary objectives in this era. Given religion's powerful emotional resonance with the masses, particularly in the Middle East, today's potent *ideology du jour*, unlike its predecessors, e.g., socialism and Baathism, may be especially deadly.

CHAPTER 5

Angry Youth:
The Fuel of Revolution

Radical anti-government scholars and clerics who want to grab political power will need to recruit to their cause the foot soldiers required for any revolutionary endeavor. The candidates will inevitably be found among the large pool of young men who are part of the disgruntled underclasses of Saudi society. That is, the cannon fodder for revolution will come from among the millions of unemployed or underemployed, bored, sexually frustrated, bitter young men roaming the vast urban spaces of the country. It is this group that will supply Islamist revolutionaries with the masses of "useful idiots," to borrow Lenin's term, needed to bring down the status quo.

In the kingdom today, two-thirds of the population are below twenty-nine years of age, and 50 percent are below the age of fifteen. Such a massive youth bulge is a political destabilizer, by definition, for any country, let alone one with the issues the kingdom faces today. Historians have long noted a close relationship between male youth booms and political instability, revolutions, wars, and upheavals,[1] such as the "civil war in medieval Portugal (1384), the English Revolution (1642–51), the Spanish conquistadores ravaging Latin America ... the French Revolution of 1789, and the emergence of Nazism in the 1920s in Germany."[2]

In Saudi Arabia, the problems of the youth bulge may be exacerbated by the suffocatingly oppressive social environment for young men. Saudi underprivileged youth today are extremely bored and frustrated. They grow up in an environment that has few of the social freedoms and entertainment opportunities available to youth even in other Muslim countries. The Wahhabi religious establishment obsessively controls their social space, so entertainment, legitimate or illegitimate, is virtually nonexistent. Mixing with the opposite sex and going to cinemas, social clubs, etc., which are key areas of interest for young men all over the world, are far beyond their reach. Unlike their richer countrymen, they cannot travel abroad to indulge freely in more worldly pleasures. For such young men who have limited financial resources and, importantly, for whom the hope of an early marriage is dashed because of its high cost, observing their more privileged brethren on social media

---

[1]   Ajay Kapur, Ritesh Samadhiya, and Umesha de Silva in a 2014 study for Bank of America Merrill Lynch.

[2]   Gwynn Guilford, "Angry Young Men Are Making the World Less Stable," *The Atlantic* (March 11, 2014), accessed July 26, 2014, http://www.theatlantic.com/international/archive/2014/03/angry-young-men-are-making-the-world-less-stable/284364/; Michael S. Arnold, "Young. Male. Explosive?" *The Wall Street Journal* (March 19, 2014), accessed August 17, 2014, http://blogs.wsj.com/economics/2014/03/19/young-male-explosive/.

traveling and indulging in all worldly pleasures can drive them to insane levels of frustration.

The impact of sexual frustration on young men was recently studied and reported on in a paper entitled "How Testosterone Drives History," which is largely based on research carried out by an Austrian academic, Karin Kneissl, in her book *Testosteron macht Politik* (*Testosterone Makes Politics*). Kneissl argues that for young males, testosterone is the substance that collects all the frustrations generated from different areas of life and focuses those frustrations on a single foe or target. She says that the main source of frustration channeled in this way is sexual and that it produces a sexuality that has no outlets. She goes on to explain that this was very much a driver in the Arab Spring revolutions, which were joined by young Muslim men who lived under a very strict social code (albeit one that was liberal by Saudi standards) that forbade sex outside of marriage—and yet the cost of marriage itself was simply beyond their means. With no legitimate outlets to release such intense sexual frustration,[3] she concludes, violence and rebellion can easily erupt.[4]

---

[3]   Omar Saghi, "Islam, Patriarchy and the State: How Sexual Repression Corrupts Society," *Worldcrunch* (June 6, 2012), accessed October 28, 2014, http://www.worldcrunch.com/islam-patriarchy-and-state-how-sexual-repression-corrupts-society/culture-society/islam-patriarchy-and-the-state-how-sexual-repression-corrupts-society/c3s5568/#.VE_HGfntj0c.

[4]   Fanny Jimenez, "How Testosterone Drives History," *Worldcrunch* (July 20, 2012), accessed July 26, 2014, http://www.worldcrunch.com/world-affairs/how-testosterone-drives-history/c1s5889/#.U7aRsRZjods%23ixzz36UzRSDls.

The even more rigorously suppressed energy of sexually frustrated young Saudi men has been held in check, so far, by the repressive machinery of the Wahhabi establishment, which presents its version of Islam as the answer to any and every frustration. The ulema constantly lecture the youth, telling them that stronger faith and devotion to Islamic rituals is the answer for all their needs and frustrations. To drive home that point, they have organizations like the Commission for the Prevention of Vice and Promotion of Virtue that are specifically focused on keeping these young people in line. This particular organization operates with full government sanction and has an enormous budget and access to the full panoply of modern police technology. It can also demand—and get—police support to carry out its activities, which mostly revolve around roaming city streets and looking for any public deviation from the strict behavioral code of Wahhabism. Inevitably, its main targets become these bored and frustrated young men, who are then arrested, incarcerated, and punished for any transgressions.

Furthermore, economics may exacerbate this problem, as economist Vishnu Varathan of Mizuho Bank has argued: "Also important is an economy's starting point. Youth born into a wealthier society who see their prospects dimming might be more frustrated and potentially dangerous" than those born in emerging Asia, where "economies can still look forward to years of catch-up growth."[5]

---

5   Arnold, "Young. Male. Explosive?"

Indeed, Saudi Arabia's middle-class and lower-middle-class youths' awareness of the "oil wealth" of their country, coupled with their increased awareness of the privileges accorded to the ruling class, leads them to want *their* share of that wealth, irrespective of any particular effort or contribution on their part. As members of a "rich" Saudi oil state, many of them expect access to its wealth with a minimum of effort and no hard work. They don't buy the argument that they need to work hard and sacrifice their comfort in exchange for more money, since they see that their more privileged countrymen are rewarded generously for making no effort other than being born into privilege.

This anger was vividly spelled out in a YouTube video posted on March 22, 2014, by an angry young Saudi man from the large Dosari tribe. Boldly identifying himself on the screen with his national ID card, the young man addressed the king directly, complained about his low salary and the high cost of living, and then demanded, in a disrespectful tone (unprecedented in Saudi society for a subject publicly addressing his monarch), that the king "give [the people] some of this oil money that [the king] and [his] family have all taken, or else." Such a public affront to royal prestige was previously unheard of in the kingdom. The clip instantly went viral, was viewed over 1.5 million times, and was subsequently emulated by many other equally angry young men in social media clips that made a similarly strong impact.[6] This man and

---

6   Abdullah al-Ghamdi followed in a YouTube video clip with a similar message and received 736,000 views. He was followed by a medical

his emulators were immediately arrested and incarcerated. But his attitude, boldness, and anger, and that of the dozen or so copycats who followed him, were palpable and should probably be seen as a strong indicator of the prevailing attitude among this cross-section of society rather than as the stance of a group of non-representative outliers, which many among the ruling elite would rather believe them to be.

Yet despite all this, public demonstrations of any consequence have simply not taken place in the country. Karen Elliott House, in one of the more insightful books written about the kingdom recently, wonders why public protests have not occurred. She attributes the absence of public protest in Saudi Arabia to a cultural and social environment that encourages conformity and even timidity in its people—what she calls "the somnolence of Saudi society itself":

> Notwithstanding the occasional terrorist who blasts onto the world stage, the [Saudi] society has been overwhelmingly passive, imbued from birth with a sense of obedience to God and ruler and with customs of conformity such that only the rarest of Saudis steps outside the strict social norms to leave his place in the labyrinth that divides Saudis one from another.[7]

---

doctor, Abdul-Rahman al-Asiri, whose clip garnered 1.5 million views, and others. See http://english.al-akhbar.com/node/19300.

[7] Karen Elliott House, *On Saudi Arabia: Its People, Past, Religion, Fault Lines—and Future* (New York: Vintage Books, 2013).

While this "somnolence" has certainly been a key facet of Saudi society to date, emerging indicators show that the Saudi state's reliance on an indefinite continuance of this somnolence may be unwise. French researcher Pascal Menoret, who spent years in close contact with youths on the streets of Riyadh, studied the psychology of these young men in his interesting and well-researched book *Joyriding in Riyadh: Oil, Urbanism, and Road Revolt.*[8] He saw in the phenomenon of rebellious joyriding known as "tafheet" (dangerous and illegal drifting in stolen cars) that is spreading among young Saudi males the beginnings of a tendency to publicly challenge authority. He also saw in their pursuit of physical danger a sign of their potential for political violence. He writes about a young man called Rakan: "To him, joyriding was the tree that hid the forest of social despair and urban dereliction, the tip of an iceberg of poverty and violence that was rarely reported on." Menoret goes on to state, "No amount of storytelling could romanticize the misery of the Riyadh underclass and the suffering that were both prompting joyriding and elicited by it." He quotes figures from a study by Saudi criminologist Salih al-Rumayh who, in a survey of middle and high school students in Riyadh, Jeddah, and Dammam, discovered that one out of every five Saudis between fifteen and nineteen years of age was in one way or another engaged in illegal joyriding. These young men roaming the streets of Saudi cities and risking their lives in a prohibited and

---

8   Pascal Menoret, *Joyriding in Riyadh: Oil, Urbanism, and Road Revolt* (New York: Cambridge University Press, 2014).

dangerous activity, playing a game of cat-and-mouse with authorities, could quickly morph into violent mobs if they sensed a weakness in government authority.

The thousands of Saudis playing a leading role in fighting with jihadi groups in Syria, Iraq, and Yemen are additional indicators of a potentially rebellious and non-somnolent youth. The prominent role that Saudi youth have played in international jihad has been evident from the days of the US-supported insurgency against the Soviets in Afghanistan to the attacks of 9/11 and beyond. Saudi journalist Jamal Khashoggi in a tweet posted on August 4, 2014, attached a list he had received of suicide bombers who had died in missions for the Islamic State in Iraq and Syria. Of the fifty-two suicide bombers listed, thirty-two of them, i.e., over 60 percent, were Saudi citizens.

The "blowback" threat that these jihadi wars pose to Saudi Arabia cannot be underestimated. To begin with, both ISIS and al-Qaeda, as well as other jihadi groups, have the Saudi kingdom in their crosshairs because any Islamist group's ambition to lead the Muslim ummah (world), by definition, requires control of the holy cities of Mecca and Medina and the prestige associated with that position and role, most particularly for any group aspiring to the Caliphate of Islam (ISIS has such an aspiration). Osama bin Laden's ultimate goal was always to overthrow Al Saud, and now ISIS seems to share that goal—a multitude of messages and statements have said as much—although ISIS's Iraqi-dominated leadership seems focused on first securing its home base in Iraq and Syria. ISIS, in particular, as the most potent player in the jihadi space today—and now that it has a physical border with the Saudi kingdom (a result of its occupying the Anbar Province of Iraq)—has to be seen as an imminent threat to the kingdom. With its base of supporters in the kingdom and a not insubstantial number of Saudis playing leadership roles for ISIS in the Iraqi and Syrian theaters, the organization could easily try and move into the kingdom if an uprising of its supporters within Saudi Arabia erupted. The Anbar border, only a few hours away from the Qasim region, is in the heartland of Najd, the emotional heartland of Wahhabism, where many observers assume it has a bedrock of sympathizers. From Qasim to the Saudi capital, Riyadh, the distance is only a couple of hours by car. Given the speed and mobility of ISIS fighters (in their favored mode of transport: four-wheel trucks and vans), such distances could easily be covered in one night.

That such ideas are percolating among the fighters of ISIS is clear. A YouTube video that came out in 2013 and showed a group of Saudi fighters in Syria was particularly telling. Sitting around a campfire, they sang a poetic song calling for the fall of the "apostate" Bashar al-Assad and then, interestingly, for the "liberation" of Al-Ha'ir, which is the "Bastille" of Saudi Arabia where most of the political prisoners are held. It was one among many indicators that Saudi fighters in Syria, Iraq, and Yemen have their eyes clearly set on revolution back home.

A clear marker also presented itself in July 2014, with the Saudi public's reaction to the arrival of ISIS on the borders of Saudi Arabia after these Islamists had "liberated" Anbar Province, Iraq. Research on Twitter showed that the majority of tweets supporting ISIS at that time were actually coming from *within* Saudi Arabia.[9] This despite the fact that ISIS has generated a lot of opposition within the Islamist community, where it has been viciously criticized for its excess and fanaticism, which clerics, both mainstream and even in the jihadi opposition, see as damaging to the cause of Islam. That ISIS still retains a strong appeal among Saudi youth, despite extensive Islamist hostility toward its extreme behavior, would seem to indicate that what appeals to these youth is not so much the particular ideology of ISIS but simply the fact that *it has been the most successful, so far, in the game of breaking down the walls of the status quo*—first in Syria, and then in Iraq, and then, maybe, even in Saudi Arabia. These youths will probably support any group emerging from the Islamic State or elsewhere that shows such revolutionary potential.

The dangerous allure of violence for Saudi Arabia's bored and frustrated young men can be very strong. As former recruits of al-Qaeda have noted, the group "sees young men as easy prey," even ones who are not devout.[10] Yet as a US Army psychological operations officer argued in a 2010 study of thousands of al-Qaeda recruits, "Rather than be recruited, young men actively seek out al-Qaeda and its associated movements," looking for an "outlet for their

---

[9]   Levy, "Could Saudi Arabia Be the Next ISIS Conquest?"
[10] Rawya Rageh, "Ex-Militants: al-Qaida Preys on Young Men," Associated Press (September 21, 2004).

frustration," "status" and "recognition," and "thrill" and "adventure."[11] Indeed, becoming a rebel with a gun brings a young man instant status and respect and allows him to plunder and destroy the envied rich. It even creates opportunities to gratify his sexual desires. The many young men who join the jihad in Syria and Iraq should be enough of an indicator of this new type of young Saudi. These men are instantly elevated in status, often from the margins of society to leaders, with the prestige instantly conferred upon gun-toting warriors. Suddenly, they become people of consequence. They expect to be and are appropriately rewarded for that role, materially, psychologically, and even sexually. The sad stories of the men of the Islamic State in Syria and Iraq who have been reported as demanding that unmarried women in areas under their control subject themselves to the "jihad" of marriage, which is little more than rape sanctified by their self-serving and twisted religious interpretation, are all too frequent. The allure of all this for underprivileged Arabian youth is intoxicating and should not be underestimated.

These disgruntled young men may not by themselves make a revolution. It will probably take charismatic leaders to make a revolution, but the opposition movements of today do not lack for such leaders. In fact, many candidates are already aspiring to such a role, from people like the London-based exile Dr. Saad al-Faqih, the head of Islah, a Saudi

---

[11]   John M. Venhaus, "Why Youth Join al-Qaeda," *United States Institute of Peace,* Special Report 236 (May 2010), accessed December 12, 2014, http://www.usip.org/sites/default/files/SR236Venhaus.pdf.

dissident organization, to the many hard-core Saudi jihadi leaders that the wars in Syria, Iraq, and Yemen are producing. These political entrepreneurs are already hard at work looking for the trigger needed to provoke these youth to break down their barrier of fear of authority and unleash their suppressed energy in an orgy of violence.

CHAPTER 6

The Mystique of State Power

The question of why public political protests in the kingdom have been few and the number of participants has been limited (with the exception of protests in the Shiite Eastern Province) begs an answer.[1] "Somnolence," for example, was clearly on display at the height of the Arab Spring in March 2011 after the Saudi opposition called for a "day of rage" across the country and yet hardly any protestors showed up. While one answer would be simply to assume total public

---

[1] A point of interest here is that the capital city Riyadh was purposefully laid out (in the 1960s by the Greek firm Doxiadis Associates) in a manner designed to make mass political protests difficult. To this purpose, wide avenues and a spread-out, low-rise urban architecture were seen as ideally suited to impeding high concentrations of people from assembling quickly and also to providing security forces with quick and easy access to all sectors of the city (Menoret, *Joyriding in Riyadh*, 1,553). Such thinking builds on the work of Frenchman Baron Haussmann, who, in 1860, planned the "new" Paris for his emperor, Napoleon III, to "prevent a recurrence of the kind of unrest that affected the city for generations. He laid out wide, straight boulevards that just happened to be one cavalry squadron wide (rather handy in the event of riots). He imposed architectural codes that ... made it harder for demonstrators to put up barricades between buildings. Haussmann effectively 'facilitated state control of the capital'" (David Kilcullen, *Out of the Mountains: The Coming Age of the Urban Guerrilla* [New York: Oxford University Press, 2013], 20).

satisfaction with the status quo, a more thoughtful answer might be that protesters were held back by that intangible force: the fear of state power present in the mind of the common person, a mystique that is enhanced by the aura and stature of traditional rulers, what Arabs call "hayba." The Saudi commoner remains in awe of, intimidated by, and respectful of the state, assuming that it is omnipotent. Such an impression is difficult to measure scientifically and can only be assessed anecdotally, but it seems to be stronger in monarchies where the legitimacy of traditional rule is more deeply entrenched in people's consciousness. This may be due to a deep-seated respect and awe for traditional rulers that commoners have inherited over generations but that modern republican and military rulers have not been able to implant as successfully into their people's consciousness. This may explain why Arab monarchies have been able to ride out the Arab Spring so far.

Yet even this type of traditional view of monarchical state power may be at risk of being shaken as young Saudis become more politically conscious and aware of the world around them and remember observing other supposedly omnipotent Arab states fall. Egypt, Tunisia, Libya, and other Arab states were all known for having ruthless security establishments that had kept their rulers in power for decades. The sudden collapse of those rulers alerted the Arab masses to the fact that state power may not be that awe-inspiring after all.

Young people in Saudi Arabia are also witness to the rapidly increasing strength and success of the jihadi non-state actors around them in Iraq, Syria, Gaza, and Yemen. Jihadis in these countries are not only standing up to and sometimes defeating powerful local governments but are also even sometimes able to resist powers like Israel and America. The emergence of new, powerful revolutionary forces that can take on these established status quo powers is capturing the imagination of youths across the kingdom and the region.

Dissidents such as Saad al-Faqih are intensely focused on this point. Faqih holds regular lectures on YouTube to argue his case. One of the main points he constantly stresses to his followers is that the Saudi state is not as powerful as they think it is and that they should not be intimidated by it. What holds people back from public protest, he repeats time and again in obvious frustration, is nothing more than their own "barrier of fear," not the actual power of the state.

Faqih's exasperation with this issue is indicative of the state's persistent hayba. That it may be slowly fading, however, can be gleaned from the increasingly disrespectful comments about the royal family that are spreading on social media, many of them posted anonymously, but also a not insignificant number of them accompanied by the commenters' actual names.

It would seem only logical that this process will inevitably lead someone to test the coercive power of the Saudi state at some opportunity. If that happens, then the government may be presented with a challenge, given that the coercive power at the disposal of the Saudi state may actually be quite limited.

The Kingdom of Saudi Arabia is not a classic Arab police state. Traditionally, it has used a minimum of coercion and a maximum of persuasion and bribery to pacify its enemies. It has nothing resembling the brutal police-state infrastructure of a Baathist Syria or Iraq, a Nasserite Egypt, or a post-independence Algeria, Morocco, or Jordan. In fact, Saudi Arabia has only begun to develop effective police-state capabilities in the last decade in response to the al-Qaeda terrorist attacks inside the kingdom. Even here, the government never took the road of extreme brutality that Saddam or Bashar al-Assad habitually traveled. Instead, it always looked to find consensual ways to bring its enemies back into the fold. While today the Saudi state incarcerates thousands of political prisoners, it has always avoided the traditional Arab police-state approach of butchering its enemies.

This long-standing and calculated policy concerning the use of physical coercion recognizes the structure of the kingdom as a tribal society and the fact that Saudi Arabia's military and security forces do not have any unique racial or sectarian tie that binds them to the Al Saud in the same way that, say, the minority Alawite-dominated Syrian military is bound to the Assad family in Syria as members of that same minority sect. In Syria, the Alawite troops realize that if the regime falls, then they and their families, as members of the same minority, will pay a terrible price at the hands of a victorious Sunni majority. Therefore, they fight to the death for the regime. In Saddam's Iraq, following a similar logic, security forces were populated by the Sunni minority and, for the president's closest protection, by fellow tribesmen from his home region around the town of Tikrit. In Saudi Arabia, the soldier, a member of the majority Sunni community, has none of that "superglue" to bind him to his rulers. He knows that he can outlive the Al Saud and that their fall will probably have no dire implications for him or his family. In fact, junior officers may even see the fall of the royal family as opening the possibility for their own advancement. In the same vein, Saudi troops are highly unlikely to shoot at their own people if called upon to do so. These troops are part of the mainstream population and would be very reluctant to turn on their own kind for the sake of the regime or ruling order.

Even the members of the Saudi National Guard, which is spoken of as the royal family's "Praetorian Guard" and some of whose bedouin grandfathers fought for the Al Saud in founding the kingdom, have none of the same impulses that their forefathers had. The ideology that King Abdul-Aziz used to convince the people of Najd to fight for him in establishing the kingdom is no longer applicable or relevant. At that time, as described previously, these people were very successfully indoctrinated to believe that fighting for the Al Saud was essentially "God's work."

Today, it would be much more difficult for the state to successfully classify all of its enemies as deviants from the true path of Islam. This time around, many competing voices would loudly and aggressively dispute this narrative, arguing instead that overthrowing the Al Saud is the "true Islamic duty." Today, such conflicting arguments would be falling on the ears of people who are no longer insulated like their grandfathers were; they are now literate and exposed to the world around them. It will be a challenge to manipulate them as easily as before.

A confirmation of the idea that coercive power is unlikely to work against the mainstream Saudi population can perhaps be seen in the fact that the only time coercive force has actually been used in modern times was, and still is, against the Shia minority in the Eastern Province. The government is able to do this because the Shia are not represented in the security forces and because the nation's troops (and people) have been indoctrinated by Wahhabism to see the Shia as "the other"—and a hostile other at that.

An example of the tenuousness of coercive power in the hands of a state is found in what happened to the late shah of Iran. He had a fearsome internal security apparatus and a powerful army and Imperial Guard, all equipped and trained to the highest standards. When the time came, however, for them to take on their own people, the Iranian masses, these troops melted away in no time. This included the "formidable" Imperial Guard, a force that was supposedly fanatically loyal to the shah. While there are obvious complexities to this narrative that cannot be addressed here, the crucial point is that the rank-and-file members of the security forces had no special bond to the Pahlavis that would have made them *associate their own survival* with that of the Iranian dynasty. The rank and file realized that they could outlive the shah and that his removal would not hurt them. Once they sensed that the throne had weakened and would no longer be able to subject them to punishment for deserting, they dispersed—and the shah's rule collapsed. A sudden collapse of coercive state power amid similar circumstances has happened time and again throughout history: in Russia with the tsar's army in 1917, and in the last days of the Qing dynasty (1644–1911) in Imperial China, among many other examples.[2] More recently, the

---

[2]   On the Russian Revolution, see Richard Pipes, *The Russian Revolution* (New York: Knopf, 1990), and on the fall of the Qing Dynasty, see Michael Gasster, "The Republican Revolutionary Movement," in *The Cambridge History of China*, ed. John King Fairbank et al., vol. 11, part 2 (Cambridge: Cambridge University Press, 1980), 463–534. Pipes's description of the "sudden shift of sentiment on the part of the most illiberal elements of Petrograd society—the right-wing officers, gendarmes, policemen—who only a few days before were pillars of the monarchy" recalls the Iranian case (289). Also relevant is his description of how neither side in the brewing conflict sensed the "political significance" of the February 1917 demonstrations precipitating the revolution. Here, Tsar Nicholas's monarchy suffered from a communication failure similar to that in Saudi Arabia, as lower-ranking regime members deliberately "soften[ed]" the severity of the revolutionary events taking place in reports to the monarch (276). According to Gasster, "Support for the Chi'ng [regime], little shaken by earlier uprisings, suddenly evaporated in 1911. A few small incidents developed rapidly into new patterns, larger movements, and finally a republic." Significantly, the "decisive elements in the coalition of 1911" were not the lower-class masses but rather the "soldiers, particularly those in the New Army, and the 'new gentry,' especially those in the provincial assemblies, self-government associations, and investors' groups" (506–07).

failure of the security forces to fight to the death for President Ben Ali of Tunisia and President Mubarak of Egypt also comes to mind.

Gauging the popularity of the Saudi government today is difficult because no independent avenues exist for people to voice their opinions and be measured scientifically.[3] Gallup, YouGuv, and Burson-Marsteller,[4] three credible organizations, have polled Saudi Arabian citizens' attitudes toward the state and have found very high levels of support for the government—levels that have, in some cases, been described by the pollsters as regional "outliers." A telephone poll, for example, found that 95 percent of Saudis support the government.[5] While such polling has even been carried out in face-to-face interviews, its accuracy must still be questioned. The problem with these types of polls in a country like Saudi Arabia is that people have no prior experience with polling and also have no way of trusting that the information they provide will be held in confidence and not turned over to the government

---

3   On the "unique challenge" of public-opinion polling in Saudi Arabia, see David Pollock, "Saudi Arabia by the Numbers," *Foreign Policy* (February 12, 2010), accessed August 19, 2014, http://www.foreignpolicy.com/articles/2010/02/12/saudi_arabia _by_the_numbers. For a broader study of the difficulties involved in polling in the Arab world, see Pollock, *Slippery Polls: Uses and Abuses of Opinion Surveys from Arab States* (Washington: Washington Institute for Near East Policy, 2008).

4   ASDA'A Burson-Marsteller Arab Youth Survey (April 7, 2014), accessed July 31, 2014, http://arabyouthsurvey.com/wp-content/ themes/arabyouth-english/downloads/AYS-Deck-en.pdf.

5   Pollock, *Slippery Polls*, 15–16.

to be used against them. Consequently, any conclusion reached from the polling data showing that the Saudi government is highly popular among its people is something that needs to be taken with a big grain of salt. David Pollock, an analyst at the Washington Institute for Near East Policy, in an article in *Foreign Policy Magazine* entitled "Saudi Arabia by the Numbers," specifically addressed this question: "There are two sets of practical difficulties that limit pollsters working in this conservative and tightly controlled country: political or cultural constraints, and special sampling challenges." The former include the suspicion with which telephone polls are viewed, the difficulty of finding local interviewers for in-person interviews, and the limited access of even these interviewers to women. As Pollock explains, "In such a traditional society, and one where opinion polls are so rare, few people chosen at random would invite a total stranger into their house and answer his nosy questions—and even fewer women would agree to do so."[6] These cultural challenges make it nearly impossible to obtain a fair sampling of Saudis.

The problem, however, with such rosy polls is that rulers generally need little encouragement to believe that their people love them, so the results of these polls tend to be made quickly available to them by parties eager to transmit "good news," a step that only reinforces the ruling class's complacency.

---

6   Pollock, "Saudi Arabia by the Numbers."

Having said this, it is also logical to assume that the not insubstantial Saudi middle class, the majority of whom are employed by the government, recognize that they have something worth preserving in the status quo. They see the chaos of the Arab Spring all around the region and understand the terrible price their neighbors are paying for revolution. The collapse of the Libyan, Syrian, Iraqi, and Yemeni states and the turmoil in Egypt post–Arab Spring are vivid reminders, if the Saudi people have any doubt about the price of revolution. Saudi Arabia's citizens are, after all, hardly in a desperate state like the Palestinians of Gaza or the Sunnis of Syria and Iraq, who have limited, and sometimes hardly available, access to basic services and opportunities. At the end of the day, Saudi citizens enjoy significant benefits from their government and, from this, have built a life that is clearly worth preserving. To this end, the government has, since the Arab Spring in 2011, considerably increased its spending to stimulate economic activity. This includes increasing government salaries, particularly for the security forces; introducing unemployment and other social benefits; making subsidized housing loans and grants more widely available; and increasing the number of students eligible for generous scholarships to study abroad. With oil prices high and government coffers overflowing, conscious efforts are being made to spread the wealth as widely as possible. Given all this, it is not a stretch of logic to assume that, at the very least, a wide swath of Saudi people, maybe even the majority, would resist any effort to shake domestic political stability.

A passive majority, however, can rarely, if ever, hold back a revolution. The change agents throughout history have generally been radical aggressive minorities who have the passion, drive, courage, and violent disposition to go out and take on the status quo. In Russia, the Bolsheviks, whose base of support was less than 1 percent of the population (no more than thirty thousand people),[7] were the ones who ultimately succeeded in taking power. They did so because they were the boldest and most ruthless[8] among the many elements that were competing for power at that time in Russia. As one scholar of revolutions has put it, "Even revolutionary movements that succeed are based on a small percentage of the total population. A revolution involves minorities fighting minorities. And if the revolutionaries have any advantage over the loyalists, it probably begins with the revolutionaries' greater *intensity* of commitment to their cause."[9]

---

[7] Thomas H. Greene, *Comparative Revolutionary Movements: Search for Theory and Justice*, 3rd ed. (Englewood Cliffs: Prentice Hall, 1990), 75.

[8] The Bolsheviks were, in Richard Pipes's words, "a tightly organized conspiracy." Of the October 1917 revolution, he wrote, "October was a classic coup d'état, the capture of governmental power by a small minority, carried out, in deference to the democratic conventions of the age, with a show of mass participation, but without mass engagement" (Pipes, *The Russian Revolution*, 385).

[9] Greene, *Comparative Revolutionary Movements*, 74. The author cites, in addition to the Russian case, the case of Algeria ("The Algerian rebellion was initiated in 1954 by no more than 500 men"), Cuba ("Some authorities put the maximum size of Castro's army at ... less than 2,000"), the United States ("The Continental Army managed to enlist only about one man for every sixteen of fighting age"), and Germany ("Prior to the Nazis' capture of power in 1933, party members constituted only 0.02% of the population"), among others (74–75).

That radical Islamic political "entrepreneurs" can succeed at instilling this type of intensity in a number of frustrated Saudi youth and then marshaling them into a revolutionary force is hardly inconceivable. Here, the simple majority of people, the middle class in favor of the status quo, will be of little help to the state, as they will probably just lie low and focus on protecting themselves and their families.

Moreover, this generation of Al Saud is unlike their predecessors: the generation of King Abdul-Aziz, who was a fighter, a man with the scars of battle all over his body to prove his iron mettle, or even King Faisal, who fought and conquered territory and was informed by that experience. This generation has been softened by seventy-five years of peace and prosperity. They may have difficulty dealing with the hardened, borderline-savage elements that the extremist jihadi movement is producing these days.

CHAPTER 7

The Price of a Saudi Collapse

History has consistently shown us the enormous price paid by the common people, not just the ruling elites, for the collapse of a developing country's ruling order. Such revolutions have done little more than remove one indulgent ruling class and replace it with another ultimately equally corrupt class while subjecting the masses to decades of pain and suffering. It would be illogical to expect that such a collapse in Saudi Arabia would turn out to be any different. In fact, every indicator shows that a destruction of the only governing institution in existence today, the House of Saud, would be cataclysmic for the country and its people, and very damaging to the global economy.

Saudi Arabia today has no independent institutions (with potential governing capability) to speak of—no political parties, no independent judiciary, not even an army with an independent institutional culture such as the Pakistani, Egyptian, and Turkish armies have—to even attempt to hold the country together in the case of revolution. The only other national institution, the Wahhabi ulema, will surely also fragment as those ulema accused of upholding the old order are themselves overthrown by the multitude of extremist rebel ulema who will emerge vying for the leadership of the Wahhabi flock, each striving to outdo the others in extremism and brutality.

In the absence of other institutions that can replace the House of Saud, the country would probably fragment in multiple ways. Geographically, it may fragment along historic fault lines, between the main regions that King Abdul-Aziz conquered and merged into his kingdom in 1932: the Hejaz with its holy cities of Mecca and Medina, the Al Hasa region (in the Eastern Province) with its oil-producing assets and large Shia population, and the south of the country with its historical links to Yemen.

The people's historic resentment of being dominated by the people of Najd, which fact is associated with the arrival of Saudi rule, would likely be rekindled and used to drive the process of fragmentation. The Najdis, to which group the Al Saud belong, today hold a position of clear prominence in the country. They hold most key senior positions, not only in the bureaucracy but also in the military, and almost exclusively control the top echelons of the Wahhabi establishment. As regional kinsmen of the Al Saud, Najdis have very clearly benefited from their proximity to power.

In the earlier days of the Saudi state, the Hejazi urban class played a relatively prominent role in helping the Al Saud govern the country, given that they constituted the most educated and sophisticated group available in Saudi Arabia at that time, but their role has gradually been whittled away in recent decades to become virtually insignificant today. That this engenders bitterness among some Hejazi elements is unquestionable.

Another fault line is with the people of the south of the kingdom in the regions of Al Baha, Asir, Jizan, and Najran. These southerners are even less represented in the circles of Saudi power than the Hejazis, yet they populate the rank and file of the army, security forces, and domestic intelligence apparatus.

Additionally, the Sunni–Shia sectarian fault line now spreading across the Levant and Iraq is already extending down into the Saudi Eastern Province with its oil wealth and large Shia population centers, its proximity to majority-Shia Bahrain, and its consequent susceptibility to Iranian influence and interference. The Shia population is boiling with resentment against the Saudi state and has been doing so for decades. After all, Wahhabi thinking, as a doctrinal principle, demonizes the Shia. As a result, the Saudi Shia, while not subjected to open persecution, have always endured the status of second-class citizens in the kingdom. Inspired by the Khomeini revolution, they revolted in the early 1980s and were put down by force. They have recently started to protest again following the Arab Spring, and, again, the full coercive might of the state is being brought against them. Thus primed for revolution, they will surely be the first fault line to crack and will inevitably seek Iranian help to fight for "independence" and attempt to take ownership of the majority of Saudi oil assets, which exist largely in the regions that have large Shia populations.

Fortunately and unfortunately alike, Saudi Arabia is a huge strategic prize, given its oil *and* the fact that it is home to the holy cities of Islam. If Lebanon, Syria, Libya, and Iraq became a competitive playground for world and regional powers, then one can certainly imagine what Saudi Arabia will become if outsiders compete, as they surely will, for its natural resources and religious mantle.

The scenario we see in Libya is, at a minimum, what would happen if the Saudi state were overthrown today. Once Gaddafi's government was overthrown, the Libyan state collapsed into its regional and tribal components, all armed to the teeth. Attempting to put it back together again as a state with a central government in control and with a monopoly on violence has been impossible so far, three years after Gaddafi's death. At the same time, Libya's oil industry has been attacked and fought over by various groups and remains threatened as production levels and distribution to international customers become highly unreliable. In Saudi Arabia, given the much larger stakes involved, such a conflict would likely bring even more devastation to the country and its people than Libya is experiencing, along with a crisis of unprecedented proportions for the global oil market and world economy.

A study produced by the Heritage Foundation in 2012 entitled "Thinking the Unthinkable: Modeling a Collapse of Saudi Oil Production"[1] evaluates the impact of a

---

[1] Ariel Cohen, Michaela Dodge, David W. Kreutzer, and James Phillips, "Thinking the Unthinkable: Modeling a Collapse of Saudi Oil Production" (April 9, 2012), *Heritage Foundation,* accessed July 16, 2014,

"complete disruption of Saudi oil production," premised on a Saudi production level of 8.4 million barrels of oil per day. In the study's scenario, which "optimistically assume[s] that repairing destroyed and damaged facilities and gradually restoring oil exports to the previous level would take approximately two years," petroleum prices immediately rise from $100 to $220 per barrel, while the American economy loses $214 billion and over one million jobs in the first year. While the dramatic increase in US shale oil production since the publication of this report will certainly mitigate the impact and may insulate the United States to a certain degree, the loss of Saudi oil and particularly the Saudi reserve excess production capability (which has served for decades to balance the global oil market) would still make the impact on oil prices, even in the United States, a dramatic one.

Furthermore, a breakdown of law and order in Saudi Arabia would put all the major oil-producing areas in Kuwait, Qatar, and Abu Dhabi within reach of hostile actors operating from within Saudi territory.

The entire Arabian oil and gas infrastructure, which consists of hundreds of potential targets, is highly combustible and vulnerable. The multiplicity of targets— oil wells, pipelines, processing facilities, refineries, storage structures, gas and LNG processing and storage sites, and

---

http://www.heritage.org/research/reports/2012/04/thinking-the-unthinkable-modeling-a-collapse-of-saudi-oil-production (data drawn from the US Energy Information Administration, www.eia.gov).

petrochemical facilities spread over a wide area from Kuwait down through eastern Saudi Arabia to Qatar and Abu Dhabi—will surely attract predatory attention like hungry wolves to sheep if the Saudi state collapses. Aside from the risk of infiltration and terrorism, the ability of today's non-state actors to deploy missiles and send them hundreds of miles to a target makes this threat even more potent. Any direct hit on any of these facilities would cause enormous explosions and fires. The staff operating these facilities, many of them foreign experts and laborers, are very aware of that risk and would hardly want to hang around and chance being incinerated. So, it is not hostility alone but even the threat of hostility that may bring the Gulf oil industry to a halt. Those having any doubt about such a scenario need look no further than the Baiji oil refinery in Iraq, which was quickly closed down after jihadi forces attacked it in July 2014.

Although it has been possible to protect the Arabian oil and gas infrastructure from terrorism, which in this case is defined as a one-off attack by a few individuals on a specific target, multiple non-state actors operating in an environment where state authority has broken down will face no such impediments or restraints. That is 50 percent of the globe's oil reserves and one-third of global daily oil production that will be put at risk should this situation materialize.

Many observers in the kingdom and abroad take the intellectually lazy route of assuming that the United States and other Western powers will "never allow this to happen," without bothering to drill down and look at such potential scenarios in a granular fashion. A revolutionary scenario in the heart of the Arabian Peninsula would give birth to many simultaneous crises and many different armed groups vying either to control these oil assets or deprive others of their benefit. These groups would have sympathizers all over the region, some working within the oil industry and others living in close proximity. There would hardly be any clear lines drawn in the sand that the United States could try to hold, and certainly not solely with airpower, the most convenient and low-cost choice for the allies today. In the event that the United States and/or its allies could muster the political will to intervene with the required ground forces, this process would take time—weeks and maybe even months—to complete. By then, considerable damage would have already been inflicted on these assets, just as was the case when Iraq put fire to the oil wells of Kuwait once defeat became a certainty.

Another facet of Saddam's invasion of Kuwait comes to mind here. Historians have noted that he gave the United States ample opportunity to destroy his invasion army when he simply stayed put in Kuwait and did not cross into Saudi Arabia when he had a chance to do so early on. Saddam had a window of nearly six months before the United States was able to finish mobilizing on the ground in Arabia to attack him. Had he crossed the Saudi border during that window, not only would he have taken over its oil assets and been able to threaten to destroy them, like he did in Kuwait, but he would have also controlled Saudi ports and airports near the Kuwaiti theater of battle. That would have forced the United States to use facilities much farther away, which would have caused enormous logistical problems. Many historians have concluded that in such a circumstance, removing Saddam without completely destroying the Saudi oil industry may well have been impossible.

The Arabian oil and gas infrastructure spread throughout the Arabian Gulf is as vulnerable as a china shop. In a revolutionary scenario, a bull, or many bulls, will ultimately get into that shop. When that happens, it will be impossible to get the bulls out without destroying all of the china.

CHAPTER 8

The Risk to the Arab Gulf States

The future of the Arab Gulf emirates, which are known, collectively with Saudi Arabia, as the Gulf Cooperation Council (GCC) members,[1] as independent states governed by their current ruling families, is inextricably tied to the future stability of the Saudi kingdom.

The kingdom, by virtue of its geography, is the foundational pillar holding up this regional dynastic political order. A collapse of the Saudi kingdom would inevitably bring down the remaining family-run monarchies of the GCC, whatever illusion anybody may have about their long-term ability to survive as stand-alone entities in the face of a hostile power replacing the Al Saud. As Robert Kaplan in his book *The Revenge of Geography* aptly reminds us, "A man-made border that does not match a natural frontier zone is always vulnerable."[2]

---

[1]   Saudi Arabia, Kuwait, Bahrain, Qatar, the United Arab Emirates, and Oman.

[2]   Robert Kaplan, *The Revenge of Geography: What the Map Tells Us about Coming Conflicts and the Battle against Fate* (New York: Random House, 2012).

97

The kingdom has a population of twenty-eight million, of which twenty million are citizens, and occupies the majority of the landmass of the Arabian Peninsula. It overshadows what are essentially city-states in the Arabian Gulf region, only one of which—Oman—has substantially more than a million citizens. Some, such as Qatar, have as little as a quarter of that number. Arguably, these city-states were able to survive as wealthy, thinly populated, independent countries after the withdrawal of their imperial British protectors in 1971 only because of the presence of a giant, friendly Saudi Arabia. With a tribal dynastic ruling family similar to those of the Gulf's city-states, Saudi Arabia had a vested interest in their political survival.

None of these Gulf states then had (or even have today) a military capable of standing up alone to a hostile land-based power or a multitude of forces coming from the Arabian Peninsula. Their vulnerability to such a predator or predators would be particularly acute since, in this case, they would not even benefit from the natural water barrier that the Persian Gulf creates between their country and Iran.

Without a large population to man an army, creating a military capable of defending their country is probably a distant objective for all of them. In these states, citizens have always avoided military service because, as part of tiny populations in countries of extraordinary wealth, they have always had other, more lucrative, and less demanding careers to choose from. Recognizing this problem, the United Arab Emirates (UAE) recently introduced mandatory military conscription for its youth, but even that will take at least a decade before it has a material impact on the country's defensive capabilities. Even then, with a population of fewer than a million citizens, the UAE's establishing a credible military deterrent against its larger neighbors will be a big challenge.

These Gulf emirates historically lived under the threat of an expansionist Saudi state, but their gradual incorporation into the British Empire, starting in the eighteenth century, drew a line in the sand, preventing successive Saudi attempts to expand at their expense. Tensions over territory and oil resources continued, however, between these emirates and Saudi Arabia well into the 1950s, but they were held in check by British military power. After the British withdrawal from the Gulf, these emirates faced a kingdom that had, by then, given up on any expansionist aims and instead saw the Gulf states as allied political entities with similar ruling systems that could fortify the then-vulnerable bloc of conservative Arab regimes against the threat of spreading republican revolutions.

This Saudi bulwark against the Arab revolutionary republican tide of that time was also essential for these young states' survival. Had Saudi Arabia fallen to a pro-Nasser military dictatorship in the 1960s, as Iraq had done in 1958, such a dictatorship would certainly not have respected the independence of the other Arab Gulf states and, in fact, would have eventually gone after them as "reactionary sheikhdoms." The Saudi–Egyptian battle for influence over and control of the region was a defining one in modern

Arab history. It began with the 1952 Free Officers coup in Egypt that brought Colonel Nasser to power and the subsequent 1956 Suez War that elevated him to the status of revolutionary hero of the Arab world. It only ended with his defeat in the 1967 war with Israel and his subsequent death in 1970. Had he succeeded in his numerous attempts to overthrow the Saudi ruling family and replace them with rulers allied to him, the resulting "revolutionary" republic in the Arabian Peninsula would have destabilized and maybe even eventually overrun the Gulf states after the British departure.

We can look to the Omani experience with the Dhofar Rebellion that started in 1962 as an example. It took the Omani government more than fifteen years to quell this rebellion, which it achieved only after securing the help of the British government and the involvement of its special forces, the SAS, in addition to Pakistani troops, and also after receiving troops and material support from the shah of Iran. The Dhofari rebels, who had initially called themselves the Dhofari Liberation Front, eventually got themselves on message with the fashionable revolutionary ideology prevalent at that time and rebranded themselves as the Popular Front for the Liberation of the Arabian Gulf (today, they would surely have repackaged themselves as Islamic jihadists). This repositioning strategy earned them the active and crucial support of a newly established revolutionary communist regime in neighboring South Yemen and of communist China, in addition to the loud support of President Nasser and the Arab "revolutionary" community. One can only imagine what might have happened if that scenario had been duplicated up and down the Gulf and was supported by a hostile expansionary revolutionary regime in place of the Saudi kingdom.

These states are so close to Saudi Arabia, ethnically and geographically, and sit on such massive hydrocarbon wealth that it is highly unlikely that any party or parties that succeed in taking control of Saudi Arabia would ever respect their independence. After all, the ideology driving any revolution in Saudi Arabia would be one that attacked the ruling-family order. Such logic would apply equally to the other Gulf states—never mind their tiny populations and the lure of their wealth.

While the United States, the United Kingdom, and France are present on the ground in the Gulf with military bases in Kuwait, Bahrain, Qatar, and Abu Dhabi, it is not clear how this military presence could prevent chaos from spreading to these states in the event that Saudi Arabia turned hostile. Insofar as any attacks or invasions are carried out by a recognized state like Iran, the presence of these bases would certainly help. The bases act as a trip wire, so a state like Iran would open itself to likely retaliation from the United States and its allies if it undertook such an overt action. The situation, however, changes dramatically if the attacking entity is a non-state actor, like a jihadi organization with no fixed home base and with allies in the emirate that are being attacked themselves. In such a confused scenario, it would be much more difficult for the United States and its allies to react appropriately. Also, the trip-wire principle would have little relevance. Here, it is unlikely that US/allied troops would come out of their bases and get into firefights on the ground with such disparate elements (which would probably include portions of the local population) in an effort to keep the ruling families in power. In any event, should local fighting break out, such scenarios will require much larger numbers of allied troops than are permanently present on these bases, most of whom, in such a crisis, would be busy focusing on protecting their own facilities, personnel, and diplomats, along with any of their citizens who happened to be residents of those emirates at the time.

Today, the United States acts as a deterrent to Iran, primarily in the waters of the Persian Gulf, and focuses on securing the safe transit of a quarter of the world's oil through the Gulf. If the United States also wanted to protect the borders of these states, starting with Kuwait and progressing down the Gulf to Oman, from invasion or even just infiltration, then this would require a vastly larger and more involved military commitment. Such a commitment would not be undertaken easily by an America that is worn out from its recent participation in conflicts in the Islamic world. A more likely scenario would be for the United States, in a desperate attempt to keep the oil flowing, to try and isolate key oil-producing facilities or areas and garrison them, but that option, by its very nature, would cover only a tiny part of the geographic area of the GCC and still leave most of these states' population centers unprotected.

My arguments here apply generally to all of the small GCC states, with the exception, maybe, of Oman, which has a larger population and much less wealth than the other states, a long history as an independent state, a more remote location with natural defensive barriers, and a better-trained and more experienced army. But even Oman, in the end, can hardly be considered a military power able to defend itself against a hostile state replacing the Saudi kingdom. On this point, the Omanis only have to remember the time when the Al Saud invaded them in the eighteenth century to appreciate their exposure. At the same time, Oman has the least valuable oil reserves of the group, so its remote location might serve it well in this instance. For Kuwait, Qatar, and Abu Dhabi in particular, their wealth would make them the primary targets of any predators emerging from the center of the Arabian Peninsula.

Given this umbilical cord of shared destiny between the Gulf states and Saudi Arabia, one would have expected these states to exert every effort to support the kingdom and help it maintain domestic stability. Surprisingly, that has not always been the case. Gulf countries have often been more concerned with emphasizing their independence from the Saudis and resisting what they see as Saudi hegemony. This has often made them look for ways to prove their independence rather than seeing the mainte-nance of Saudi stability as necessary for their very existence. Their massive oil and financial wealth obviously provides them with a strong platform from which to insist on their independence and take public steps to drive home this point to the outside world. Often, they have made foreign policy decisions that are clearly at odds with Saudi wishes. They also veto steps to increase integration among the GCC states since they fear that the GCC will become a front for Saudi hegemony.

In fact, some of them have gone as far as to take overtly hostile action against the Saudi state. Qatar even funded and used its vast media interests to promote Saudi dissidents in their attempt to overthrow the Al Saud and break up the country. Recent recordings—released by Libyan revolutionaries after the overthrow of Muammar Gaddafi and made available on YouTube—of discussions between the former emir and the former prime minister of Qatar and Gaddafi have exposed these efforts. In the recordings, both Qatari leaders clearly describe to Gaddafi their efforts to fund and promote Saudi dissidents and then express their hope that this will lead to a breakup of the kingdom. The Qatari leaders may have thought that a breakup of Saudi Arabia would result in a multiplicity of successor states replacing the one large Saudi hegemon on their border and that such an environment would be less threatening to the tiny Qatar. The dangerous implications of such a breakup, however, and the disruptive forces that it would unleash, which would hardly spare an Al Thani–ruled Qatar, appear, astonishingly, not to have been a consideration for the Qatari leadership.

Kuwait, in the 1960s, also adopted a similarly resentful and somewhat hostile attitude toward the kingdom, reflecting a desire to prove its independence and importance as a stand-alone player on the world scene. King Faisal often vented his exasperation with Kuwaiti behavior by joking that the world had three superpowers: the United States, the USSR, and Kuwait! When Saddam Hussein invaded Kuwait in 1990, its rulers, the Al Sabah, finally appreciated the importance of the Saudi state to their survival. A Saudi government hostile to the Al Sabah could have behaved very differently then, and with disastrous consequences for the Kuwaiti ruling family. Saudi Arabia could have avoided the heavy political and financial price it paid to allow the United States to operate from its territory in liberating Kuwait. Instead, King Fahd could have cut a deal with a very eager Saddam to divide Kuwait. In parallel, the Saudis would surely have been able to secure US protection against any further encroachment by Saddam. Having learned that painful lesson, the Al Sabah today openly acknowledge Saudi leadership and maintain excellent and cooperative ties with the kingdom.

Today, GCC rulers need to recognize that any regime succeeding the Al Saud will inevitably be a hostile, ambitious, and covetous Islamist regime—one that will sound the death knell for all the other Gulf sheikhdoms, regardless of any foreign alliances that they may be counting on to save them.

The structural vulnerability of tiny city-states can even be seen in the recent history of Europe. City-states like Monaco, Lichtenstein, and Andorra continue to exist independently in Europe today only because they maintain political and economic systems that are in harmony with their giant neighbors and also because they abide by those neighbors' key wishes. In 1962, Monaco, as an example, annoyed the French government by allowing French citizens to hide their wealth in the banks of Monte Carlo and thereby avoid paying taxes on it. When President de Gaulle then threatened Monaco with invasion and mobilized his troops (police, in this case) on the border, Prince Rainier, the ruler of Monaco at the time, immediately buckled and signed an agreement that essentially turned his principality into a French protectorate. Furthermore, had any of these states also sat on valuable oil or gas reserves—or had they particular strategic value to their larger neighbors—then their continued independence would have been very unlikely.

It would be unrealistic to think that any of the Gulf states could indefinitely maintain their independence against a large, hostile, land-based neighbor in the Arabian Peninsula. Their only hope in that eventuality would be to seek the protection of another neighboring power, Iran or maybe even India, but choosing such an option would, by definition, effectively end their independence.

This logic would argue for the smaller GCC states to change their current focus on emphasizing their independence from the kingdom and, instead, actively work toward a confederation with Saudi Arabia. A federal structure that also included Yemen would address the demographic imbalances prevalent now in the sparsely populated GCC states and also likely eliminate the inevitable crisis that the currently failing Yemeni state will bring upon the whole GCC, as I discuss in the coming chapter on Yemen. Finally, the process of establishing a confederation in the Arabian Peninsula would give the whole GCC ruling order a fresh boost of nation-building legitimacy with its people, as a new and much stronger state of fifty million people would be established with a solid balance of financial and human resources that would not only be economically more sustainable than the current collection of seven states, but would also be militarily far more able to credibly deter potential predators, particularly Iran.

CHAPTER 9

The Iranian Threat

Externally, a prevailing threat hovers over Saudi Arabia in the form of a politically ambitious and economically stressed Iran. The Islamic Republic's ruling Shia clergy see the Saudi Wahhabi state as an historic enemy, given the doctrinally hostile Wahhabi view of Shiism and the Shia memories of the attacks on their holy cities of Karbala and Najaf in the early nineteenth century by the Al Saud and their Wahhabi warriors.

In 1801, the Saudi Wahhabis twice besieged Najaf and violently raided Karbala, massacring thousands and destroying Shiism's most sacred shrines, those of Prophet Muhammad's son-in-law Ali and grandson Husayn.[1] Theocrats, by definition, have a strong historical memory. While analysts often talk about how China today is still informed by its historical memories of Western aggression during the Opium Wars, Iran's mullahs not only have a very strong and raw memory of Wahhabism but also are reminded of it daily by the large contemporary presence of the Saudi Wahhabi state facing them across the Persian

---

[1] Yitzhak Nakash, *The Shi'is of Iraq* (Princeton: Princeton University Press, 1994), 28.

Gulf and actively opposing their ambitions across the region. They saw this manifested in Saudi Arabia's active support of Saddam Hussein during his war with Iran, and they see it in the kingdom's ongoing battle with Iran and its allies and proxies in Syria, Iraq, and Yemen. The fact that this traditional enemy also possesses massive oil wealth and controls the Islamic holy cities of Mecca and Medina, with the associated claim to leadership of the Islamic world, only serves to color the Iranian desire for revenge with contemporary sentiments of political ambition and covetousness.

Soon after their 1979 revolution, Iran's mullahs, in their quest to spread the revolution into the Arab world, began working hard to rekindle the powerful historic flame of Arabian Shias' feelings of bitterness and anger projected at their Sunni overlords, particularly in Bahrain and the Eastern Province of Saudi Arabia. The mullahs were well aware of the status of these embittered communities and realized that playing the Shia affinity card would give them influence over the Arab Shia, which they may then have been able to utilize in their ongoing rivalry with Arabia's Sunni rulers. This was particularly interesting to the Iranians because the Shia heavily populate the oil-producing Eastern Province of Saudi Arabia. According to leading estimates, Saudi Shiites constitute between 33 and 50 percent of the population of the oil-rich Eastern Province.[2] These Shia communities, politically mobilized

---

[2] Estimates of other Shia populations in the Gulf stand at 9 percent for Kuwait, 10 percent for the United Arab Emirates, 15 percent for

since the 1960s, were inspired by the Khomeini revolution and began to entertain the idea of using Iranian power to improve their lot in Arabia. The more aggressive among them responded favorably to Iranian military training and support in establishing insurgency movements in Bahrain and Saudi Arabia.

In Saudi Arabia, the main Shia opposition group, the Shia Reform Movement, which was founded in the 1970s by religious scholar Hassan al-Saffar, restyled itself after 1979 as the Organization for the Islamic Revolution in the Arabian Peninsula. Initial activity in the early 1980s by this group and similar groups was forcefully stopped by Saudi security forces. The groups went underground afterwards, emerging on occasion to carry out terrorist attacks. For example, according to the United States, the June 1996 bombing of the Khobar Towers in Dhahran was the work of the Saudi-based Shia group "Hezbollah in the Hejaz," described by the US Department of Justice in 2001 as "inspired, supported, and directed by elements of the Iranian government."[3]

Iran's strategic ambitions in Eastern Arabia are particularly explicit in the case of Bahrain, a country to which Iranian leaders have long staked a territorial claim. Not

---

Qatar, and 3 percent for Oman. See Laurence Louër, "The Rise and Fall of Revolutionary Utopias in the Gulf Monarchies," in *The Shi'a Worlds and Iran*, ed. Sabrina Mervin (London: Saqi, 2010), 63.

[3]   Toby Jones, "Saudi Arabia," in *Militancy and Political Violence in Shiism: Trends and Patterns*, ed. Assaf Moghadam (New York: Routledge, 2012), 135–42.

only is Bahrain physically and politically close to Saudi Arabia, but also its Shia community is an extension of the Saudi Shia community, and many Saudi and Bahraini Shia consider the Eastern Province of Saudi Arabia to be part of historical Bahrain. Laurence Louër, a French academic, in her book *Transnational Shia Politics*,[4] talks about the Shia "myth of the golden age," which is prevalent in Shia popular consciousness and is eagerly propagated by activist Shiite intellectuals. In this historical golden age, the Shia of Eastern Arabia were supposedly united in one single country, Bahrain, which extended *from Basra to Oman*. Its inhabitants were called Baharna, their capital was in Al Hasa (in today's Saudi Arabia), and they had embraced Shiism since the beginning of Islam. It was a time of prosperity, social harmony, and order. That all changed, according to the narrative, when the Sunni tribes—the Al Khalifa and the Al Saud—took over the region. Significantly, the region's history with the Portuguese, the Ottomans, and the Persians has all been conveniently overlooked.

Iranian control of Bahrain would give Iran proximity to this community and considerably increase the chance of a direct Iranian threat to Saudi Arabia and its oil industry. Bahrain, in fact, would be a platform for such a threat. Hence, Saudi governments have consistently taken this issue very seriously, most recently with the military support they

---

[4]   Laurence Louër, *Transnational Shia Politics* (New York: Columbia University Press, 2008).

extended to the Bahraini government after mass anti-government demonstrations in 2011.

While the shah had dropped the issue of Bahrain following a 1971 referendum on Bahraini independence, Iran's revolutionary leaders resurrected it and added sectarian overtones. As recently as 2007, the Iranian claim created a storm when Hossein Shariatmadari, editor of the Iranian newspaper *Kayhan* and a close advisor of Iran's supreme leader, wrote that "Bahrain is part of Iran's soil."

Furthermore, Shariatmadari suggested that all the governments of the GCC countries were illegitimate and destined to be overthrown by the forces of the Islamic Revolution: "The heads of these governments ... believe, and rightly so, that the Iranian model is bound to bring about the fall of their unlawful regimes."[5] His is hardly an isolated view but is, in fact, a foundational tenet of this Iranian theocracy—one that reflects the deep, passionate, and lifelong hatred that the founder of the Islamic Republic, Ayatollah Khomeini, held toward the Saudi Wahhabi state. In his first public political step, taken in 1945, Khomeini published a polemic entitled "The Unveiling of Secrets." In it, he attacked Iranian reformers who were then striving to rid the Shia of their popular rituals and cult of saints. He described these reformers as no better than agents of the

5   Y. Mansharof and I. Rapoport, "Tension in Iran–Bahrain Relations After *Kayhan* Editor Claims Bahrain Is an Inseparable Part of Iran" (August 3, 2007), MEMRI, accessed July 29, 2014, http://www .memri.org/report/en/0/0/0/0/0/0/2314.htm.

puritanical Saudis, "the savages of Najd and camel grazers of Riyadh," as he called them.[6] After the Iranian-inspired Shia riots in Mecca during the hajj of 1987, which led to a bloody confrontation with Saudi security forces, Khomeini compared "these vile and ungodly Saudis" to "daggers that have always pierced the heart of the Moslems from the back." He furthermore saw "the contaminated hands of the United States and Israel emerging from the sleeves of [the] devious ... ringleaders of Saudi Arabia and the traitors to the two holy shrines."[7] And Khomeini's last will and testament, read aloud by his successor, Khamenei, before the Assembly of Experts in June 1989, alleged the "illegitimacy" of the Saudi rulers in particular, whom he called "puppets" of the United States and "traitors to the greatest Divine Sanctuary, upon whom be the maledictions of Allah and His angels."[8] He accused them of "propagating an anti-Qur'anic religion that is this totally baseless and superstitious religion of Wahhabism."[9]

Khomeini's goals, according to Iranian-American scholar Vali Nasr, went far beyond mere hatred. "Tehran had an even loftier goal, however: to restore genuine Islamic rule

---

[6] James Buchan, *Days of God: The Revolution in Iran and Its Consequences* (New York: Simon and Schuster, 2013), 94.

[7] "Excerpts from Khomeini Speeches," *The New York Times*, August 4, 1987.

[8] Ruhollah Khomeini, *Imam Khomeini's Last Will and Testament* (Washington, DC: Embassy of the Democratic and Popular Republic of Algeria, Interests Section of the Islamic Republic of Iran, n.d.), 16.

[9] Ibid., 12.

to that special land with its long religious history, the Arabian Peninsula ... Khomeini was no doubt eyeing control of the kingdom as an important stepping-stone to his goal of claiming Muslim world leadership for himself and his movement."[10]

Less of a public firebrand than his predecessor, today's supreme leader, Ayatollah Khamenei, tones down the anti-Saudi rhetoric during times when making gestures of rapprochement suits Iranian political purposes, but he allows it to heat up at other times. To this end, the Iranian media continuously runs negative stories about the Al Saud.

Iran's ambitions in Arabia met a wall of resistance in the Iraq of Saddam Hussein, which provoked the Iran–Iraq War. This ambition to extend Iran's reach into Arabia, however, was rekindled with the American invasion of Iraq in 2003, the subsequent toppling of Saddam Hussein's regime, and its replacement by Shia-majority rule. In effect, the Sunni wall of resistance that Saddam had built to keep Iran out of Arabia was broken by the Americans. This not only gave Iran a new ally in the place of a powerful historic enemy but also allowed the Iranians to enlist fifteen million Iraqi Arab Shias into their anti-Saudi cause while opening the doors for Iranian operatives to infiltrate more easily the Shia communities of the Arabian Gulf, given the close ties of the Kuwaiti, Saudi, and Bahraini Shia to the Shia of southern Iraq and its holy cities.

---

[10] Vali Nasr, *The Shia Revival: How Conflicts within Islam Will Shape the Future* (New York: Norton, 2006), 151.

Today, Iran overtly and covertly utilizes the powerful and increasingly effective weapon of sectarianism to drive a wedge between Arabians, under the guise of wanting to "protect" fellow Shias in a potent and potentially successful attempt to co-opt the disenfranchised Shia minorities of Arabia into its program of political and territorial expansion.

The potency of such an Iranian threat to the Arabian ruling order depends on what tack one predicts the Islamic Republic will take going forward. Many who argue that this threat is illusory claim that the Iran of today is tired, that its people are fundamentally pro-American, and that its leaders are eager to rejoin the international community and will be careful to avoid any political or military adventurism that might hinder them from achieving that goal. The Iranian people, they argue, want to enjoy life, have iPhones, travel, etc., and are sick and tired of conflict, sacrifice, and revolutionary Islam. Consequently, the argument continues, the Iranian regime has no choice but to respond to its people's yearnings, get off its revolutionary high horse, and start delivering growth and prosperity.

The inevitable conclusion, in light of this optimistic argument, is that the Iran of the future will strive to reintegrate into the global community of nations, focus inwardly on its own economic development, and ultimately prove to be a force of stability and progress in the region. That argument, of course, presupposes that the current regime retains the option of realistically meeting its people's high expectations in the near future. This, in my view, is unlikely.

The Iran of today, by any standard of measurement, is a country that is facing serious economic difficulty and suffering from deep structural problems that will be difficult for the theocracy currently in power to address without risking its hold on power. These problems basically emanate from the destructive cost of the Iranian Revolution and its immediate aftermath of expropriating assets and transferring the management of the economy to politically reliable cadres rather than to proven technocrats. This resulted in a massive brain drain of Iranian talent to the West and was followed by the incredibly costly and destructive war with Iraq. Postwar Iran was unable to rebuild fully its economy and infrastructure because it continued to suffer punitive economic sanctions that were put in place after the US embassy hostage crisis of 1979.

These sanctions have only become more severe over time and have taken a heavy toll, particularly on the energy sector. Before the revolution, the Pahlavi regime was exporting some 6 million barrels of oil per day; the new regime has struggled to maintain exports above 3.5 million barrels.[11] In fact, Iran's output of oil and gas is at risk of permanent decline because the country lacks access to the technology, proper state-of-the-art maintenance, and the best practices needed to maintain its existing oilfields.[12]

---

[11] Fareed Mohamedi, "The Oil and Gas Industry," in *The Iran Primer*, ed. Robin Wright (Washington, DC: United States Institute of Peace, 2010), 100–04.

[12] Fareed Mohamedi, "The Oil and Gas Industry," from "The Iran Primer" (2010), *United States Institute of Peace*, accessed July 31, 2014, http://iranprimer.usip.org/resource/oil-and-gas-industry.

Some of this damage will be hard to reverse even if sanctions are lifted. Without significant new investments, Iranian production could fall even lower in coming years.[13]

The figures above hide other vulnerabilities. For example, on account of sanctions, well over 50 percent of Iran's oil revenues accumulate in semi-accessible or inaccessible accounts, which are available only "to purchase humanitarian and non-sanctionable commercial goods." As a result, the Central Bank of Iran has fewer resources to draw on when coping with economic shocks.[14] In June 2014, the US Congressional Research Service estimated Iran's accessible hard currency reserves at only $20 billion, with between $60 billion and $80 billion in inaccessible foreign accounts.[15]

With inflation fluctuating constantly, averaging more than 20 percent between 1980 and 2014, and with an increasingly unaffordable social safety net—critical to keeping the masses quiet—Iran's situation is a very difficult one.[16] The year 2013 was particularly dismal. The GDP

---

[13] Kenneth Katzman, "Iran Sanctions," Congressional Research Service (October 23, 2014), 53, *Federation of American Scientists*, accessed October 29, 2014, http://fas.org/sgp/crs/mideast/RS20871.pdf.

[14] Mark Dubowitz and Rachel Ziemba, "When Will Iran Run Out of Money?" (October 2, 2013), *Foundation for Defense of Democracies* and *Roubini Global Economics*, accessed July 30, 2014, http://www.defenddemocracy.org/media-hit/when-will-iran-run-out-of-money/.

[15] Katzman, "Iran Sanctions," 51.

[16] Indicators of Iranian inflation are drawn from "Iran Inflation Rate, 1957–2004" *Trading Economics*, accessed July 30, 2014, http://www.tradingeconomics.com/iran/inflation-cpi.

registered its first decline in twenty years, the unemployment rate rose to around 20 percent, inflation reached 45 percent by official accounting (and, in fact, may have been as high as 70 percent), and, by the end of the year, oil production had fallen to between 2.6 and 2.8 million barrels per day, much of that accumulating as unsold crude stored in tankers or onshore storage tanks.[17] To make matters worse, the Iranian government has continued to phase out a system of direct cash subsidies for fuel purchases. An embarrassing indication of the subsidy program's failure appeared in 2013 when Iran's vice president acknowledged that the official number of subsidy recipients somehow exceeded the number of people in the country.[18] His admission underscores the sheer volume of corruption in the Iranian government and economy, a problem that worsened considerably during the Ahmadinejad years (2005–13). In 2013, Iran ranked 144 out of 175 in Transparency International's Corruption Perception Index, a position it shared with Cameroon, the Central African Republic, and Nigeria, among others.[19]

---

[17] Katzman, "Iran Sanctions," 50–52.

[18] Bijan Khajehpour, "What to Do about Iran's Subsidy Reforms?" (October 16, 2013), *Al-Monitor*, accessed July 30, 2014, http://www.al-monitor.com/pulse/originals/2013/10/iran-subsidy-reforms-fuel-commodities-entitlements-cash-paid.html.

[19] "Corruption Perceptions Index 2013," *Transparency International*, accessed August 4, 2014, http://www.transparency.org/cpi2013/results.

Lifting sanctions is hardly going to solve these problems in the near future. In fact, if anything, lifting sanctions may exacerbate the government's problems by heightening the Iranian people's expectations too quickly. Should the regime try to pursue a textbook IMF approach to economic reform, it will have to relinquish the huge infrastructure of patronage upon which its core support is built. This would be a revolutionary step fraught with massive political risk. In light of this, Iran is hardly a candidate for a successful perestroika. After all, the mullahs know well what perestroika did to destroy the political career of Mr. Gorbachev and to end the USSR.

In any event, cynics would argue—irrespective of these stark economic facts—that the mullahs are hardly about to change their spots and suddenly focus on turning their country into a new South Korea. This Iranian theocracy, after all, dances to a different tune, an ideology articulated by its revered founder, Ayatollah Khomeini, which today is enthusiastically carried out by his heir, disciples, and followers. The theocracy's priorities are evidenced by the fact that the mullahs have been willing to bleed the Iranian economy dry for decades in order to fund a power-projection capability all the way from Lebanon to Iraq to Syria, sacrificing their men and their desperately scarce foreign exchange in order to do so. This is the regime that, after all, has undertaken a decades-long and enormously expensive ballistic missile and nuclear weapons program while its people continue to want for basic goods, medicine, and services.

Painfully for the Iranians, all of this has been taking place while their Arab Gulf neighbors continue to drown in oil wealth, buy and build the biggest and the best of everything, and yet struggle to spend the hundreds of billions of dollars that gush into their coffers every year. As Arabs happily flaunt their wealth, Iranians look on with resentment and envy combined with a toxic sense of racial and cultural superiority. They feel, and have always felt, instinctively entitled to lead the "Persian" Gulf and control its wealth.

The phenomenon of Iranian "exceptionalism" is well attested. Sadegh Zibakalam, a professor at Tehran University, describes as common the belief in "the inherent superiority of Iranian civilization," which is a contributing factor to Iranian leaders' "ideological crusade."[20] He explains as follows:

> Whenever Iran issues any fiery statement about our neighbors in the U.A.E., Qatar, or Kuwait, you can easily detect that they revolve around a belief that Persians are superior. Listen to our foreign minister, parliament speaker, or even mosque imams, and you will notice that derogatory tone they use and which focuses on the racial and not only the political superiority of Persians.[21]

---

[20] Sadegh Zibakalam, "Iranian 'Exceptionalism'" (January 29, 2009), *Middle East Institute*, accessed July 30, 2014, http://www.mei.edu/content/iranian-exceptionalism.

[21] Saud al-Zahed, "Hatred of Arabs Deeply Rooted in Persians, Says Iranian Intellectual" (October 9, 2011), *Al Arabiya*, accessed July 31, 2014, http://english.alarabiya.net/articles/2011/10/09/170927.html.

Proponents of this pessimistic view also look anxiously at the DNA of the Islamic Republic and its ruling class. They see ambitious theocrats soaked in an historic Shia narrative of pain and suffering, having struggled for decades to overthrow the Western-backed Pahlavi monarchy only to immediately face a hostile West (eagerly egged on by the Sunni rulers of Arabia) pushing the Iranian people toward counterrevolution and regime change. They blame Westerners and Gulf Arabs for nudging (and financing) Saddam to declare war on Iran—a war that cost Iran hundreds of thousands of its youth and destroyed its economy and infrastructure, not to mention the decades of sanctions that followed, which have bled the country dry. On top of that, Iranian leaders see themselves as facing ongoing "Wahhabi-led terrorism" against their allies: the Shia of Iraq, Lebanon, and Bahrain, and the Alawite regime of Syria. They also deeply resent ongoing Sunni rule over what they claim are disenfranchised Shia minorities in Arabia, which condition they blame on a Saudi state built on a Wahhabi ideology that not only fuels Sunni hatred of the Shia and Iran but also urges America "to cut the head off the Iranian snake."

Visitors to Tehran in recent years have consistently noted a deep, visceral Iranian ruling-class hatred of Gulf Arab leaders in general, and of the royal Saudi Wahhabi establishment in particular. The mullahs see destroying that establishment as essential, not only to settle historical scores but also to achieve Iranian Islamic leadership and realize their Persian imperial dreams in the Gulf.

The surest and most reliable way for the Islamic Republic of Iran to get access to this wealth, settle scores, and satisfy its sectarian and nationalistic imperial impulses (and maybe even survive as a regime) is to dominate or perhaps even destroy the ruling Sunni GCC dynastic order and achieve influence or some form of direct control over Arabian Gulf oil. Standing between Iran and its goal—really, its dream—is nothing but America, but only an America willing to fight Iran, if necessary. As the American will to fight clearly weakens under domestic political pressure, and as the Iranians improve their relations with the West and drive a wedge into the US–GCC alliance and now maybe even partner with America to fight Sunni jihadis, their opportunity—and with it, their hunger—for "their" empire will only increase.

Iran today faces an adversary that is militarily exposed. The GCC's expensive militaries are as yet untested, as their officers and troops have never had to fight a "real" war to test their mettle. GCC participation in the 1990 liberation of Kuwait was symbolic, as is the GCC's recent participation in allied bombings against ISIS in Iraq and Syria. While serious efforts have been undertaken in recent years, for example in the Saudi military, to upgrade human military capabilities, particularly with elite/special forces units, the success of these efforts, in the absence of a war fought (without US cover against a credible opponent), is difficult to gauge. Armies, even with the best of intentions, can rarely develop the required capabilities for combat if they have never been exposed to it before. Even countries with long military traditions and well-trained militaries become rusty and sloppy during long periods of peace. Here, the example of both Iran and Iraq in their long, vicious war against each other comes to mind. Both countries had militaries at that time (1980) that were well equipped and trained. Iraq had also participated, albeit in a limited fashion, in the 1973 Arab–Israeli War. Despite this, both militaries performed miserably in combat in the first few years of the war. They were only able to acquire the skills to fight effectively after years of heavy fighting and after learning their lessons the hard way, i.e., by suffering massive human and material losses and risking defeat. Only then did Saddam and the Iranian mullahs alike accept the practice of promoting officers on merit rather than on loyalty and allow their by then experienced officer class to make the key decisions in battle instead of permitting militarily clueless political leaders to micromanage them from above. That is, they basically learned how to wage war properly.[22]

The GCC militaries, without the benefit of such a military history or tradition and still heavily reliant on foreign advice and assistance, are unlikely to be able to deal alone with a power like Iran, a country with nearly three times the collective population of the GCC.

Iran, despite its decades-long inability to openly access Western military technology due to sanctions, is a strong and hardened military power by regional standards. It has

---

[22] Williamson Murray and Kevin D. Woods, *The Iran–Iraq War: A Military and Strategic History* (Cambridge: Cambridge University Press, 2014).

a large, motivated, and ideologically indoctrinated military. Its powerful Revolutionary Guard has acquired considerable experience and expertise in asymmetrical warfare, first in Lebanon, building and working with its client Hezbollah (fighting a first-rate military power like Israel); next in Iraq, during the days of the American occupation; and now in Syria, defending Assad, and in Iraq, fighting the Sunnis. Iran's Revolutionary Guard has also, by necessity, had to develop a not inconsiderable capability for local weapons design and production. In addition, it retains a strong political will to sacrifice its troops for a cause. Its strength is supported by a vast network of allies and agents in Arab Shia communities, starting with Hezbollah and including the Alawites and their allies in Syria, the Iraqi Shia, the Houthis in Yemen, and the under-privileged among the Gulf Arab Shia. The Iranians have a lot of cards to play with here. Iran does not need to physically conquer the Gulf with its armies to achieve its objectives. The mullahs have mastered the game of proxy control under the guise of local Shia communities and organizations.

In southern Iraq, Iran has this type of infrastructure already in place. These forces can easily cross GCC borders at the slightest provocation, in what could be packaged as a "popular" Iraqi movement of people across borders to save their distressed Shia brethren in Arabia. In such a scenario, one certain to create massive geopolitical confusion, the United States would hardly allow itself to become embroiled in what it would probably deem a Muslim civil war. Given the short distances involved between the Iraqi border and the heartland of Arabian oil, and given the presence of over two million potential Shia sympathizers in this heartland, GCC leaders can only ignore such a possibility at their own peril.

Arabian elites fail to gauge the depth of hatred that the Iranian ruling class has for them. This is not something that can be sorted out in negotiations between Saudi Arabia and Iran. Only the barrier of Saudi–GCC military power combined with serious reform to reintegrate the Shia into the Arabian political order will keep the Iranian hegemon at bay and prevent it from eventually swallowing, in one way or another, the oil-producing regions of the GCC.

Here, the integration of the Shia minority into the Saudi state has to be addressed as a matter of urgency. The Saudi state needs to realize that it is now actively competing with the Iranians for the loyalty of its own Shia citizens and that its outreach has to be more aggressive. The government should end all restrictions on Shia employment across the board and forcefully remove other, unwritten barriers that the Shia face daily in the legal and educational spaces. The Wahhabi establishment, which the government understandably fears will react in a hostile manner to such steps, has to be made to understand that losing the Saudi Shia is losing them to Iran's mullahs. They have to recognize that, in a way, the battle for the loyalty of "their" Shia may decide the future ownership of Arabia's oil region.

In turn, the argument that should be used with the Arab Shia is to remind them continuously of traditional Iranian prejudice toward the Arabs, which obviously includes Shia Arabs. Graham Fuller and Rend Rahim Francke, the latter of whom is an Iraqi Shia who was Iraq's first ambassador to the United States after the US invasion, wrote in their book *The Arab Shi'a*:

> Iran's own views of Arab Shia are complex ... Iranians on a popular level tend to look down on Arabs as a whole, to view them as primitive bedouin "locust-eaters" from the desert, as opposed to the ancient urbanized Persian culture ... "A dog in Isfahan lives better than an Arab in Arabia," goes one Persian proverb.[23]

The authors go on to note that

> Iran as a state tends to view Shiite communities in the Gulf as objects to be manipulated for Iranian State interests ... As the Soviet Union once felt free to sacrifice (or defend) the interests of Communist parties around the world, depending on the immediate tactical needs of the Soviet state, so too Iran is ready to use, or ignore, the interests of the Arab Shia depending on the immediate needs of Tehran's foreign policy. In January 1988 Khomeini issued a stunning landmark fatwa that placed the needs of the state above all others: "Our government ... has priority over all other Islamic tenets, even over prayer, fasting and the pilgrimage to Mecca." This

---

[23] Graham E. Fuller and Rend Rahim Francke, *The Arab Shi'a: The Forgotten Muslims* (New York: Palgrave Macmillan, 2001), 79.

remarkable redirection of Iran away from ideology to statecraft ... will increasingly determine Iran's approach to the Arab Shia.[24]

Yet as long as the Arabian Shia remain underdogs and perceive themselves as outcasts, they will be vulnerable to manipulation by Iran and Shia-led Iraq.[25]

The Wahhabi ulema have to be made to realize that, in addition to the fact that the ownership of "their" oil region is at stake, even their own physical safety and that of their families and community is at risk by allowing this problem to fester, thereby giving the Iranians and their Iraqi allies a pretext for intervention.

At the same time, the traditional dismissive Sunni attitude toward the Shia minorities, traditionally viewing the Shia as timid, easily intimidated subjects who will never dare to revolt, should, by now, what with the emergence of organizations like Hezbollah in Lebanon and the Quds Force of the Iranian Revolutionary Guard and its many Arab subsidiaries, be recognized as no longer realistic. The era of subservience and timidity of the Arab Shia in the face of their Sunni overlords is over. Failure to recognize this and address it successfully may well prove to be catastrophic for the Saudi state.

The government should try to redefine this issue with its Wahhabi base. It can no longer be viewed simply as an

---

[24]   Ibid., 80.
[25]   Ibid., 155.

issue of the mainstream's theological aversion to a "deviant" sect. Instead, it has to be redefined as a national security risk of considerable proportions. Taking such a step is obviously easier said than done for the Al Saud, given the passion with which the Wahhabi community dislikes Shiism and also given the growing flame of sectarianism sweeping across the region. Al Saud, if they reach out too far to the Shia, will provoke their Wahhabi base, a base that is already under threat from extremist Sunni jihadis, so they face a very tricky balancing act. A possible lubricant here can certainly be money, which the government can *pour* into Shia areas, uplifting that community and even distracting its people with the pursuit of wealth. While obviously cynical, such a strategy recognizes that money is a card that the government has in abundance these days, one that can allow it to, at least, buy time for an eventual long-term structural solution that reintegrates the Shia more fully into the state and society.

CHAPTER 10

The Yemenis Are Coming

Yemen presents another political and military danger to Saudi Arabia. A country with over twenty-five million poor people boxed in at the southern corner of the Arabian Peninsula, the rapidly failing state of Yemen is home to potential waves of desperate refugees waiting for an opportunity to walk across their rich neighbor's border.

Yemen has been a security problem for Saudi Arabia and the other Gulf states since the 1962 revolution, which saw the overthrow of its ruling royal family. This led to years of civil war that involved Saudi Arabia on the side of the royalist forces and Egypt on the side of the republican revolutionaries. When this civil war ended with Egypt's defeat in 1967, Saudi Arabia was left stuck with a miserably poor country ravaged by war on its doorstep.

As part of a wise and sustainable approach to dealing with this problem, King Faisal then allowed Yemeni workers virtually unlimited access to the Saudi labor market and even extended to them labor rights similar to those enjoyed by Saudi citizens. This created millions of jobs for Yemenis and contributed massively to Yemen's economy. While this policy was somewhat unpopular in Saudi Arabia (where low-income Saudis justifiably saw the Yemenis as competition), it wisely recognized the more serious long-term danger to the kingdom's security posed by a poor, hungry, unstable Yemen.

Unfortunately, this wisdom came to a screeching halt with the Iraqi invasion of Kuwait and with Yemeni leader Ali Abdullah Saleh's open support of Saddam Hussein. The Saudi government immediately retaliated by withdrawing the special Yemeni labor privileges, effectively expelling most Yemeni laborers from the country in what would prove to be an unfortunate decision with devastating consequences for the Yemeni economy.

While the discovery and export of oil beginning in 1986 gave the Yemeni economy a temporary boost, corruption and inefficiency mitigated any long-term structural benefits that such a windfall could have brought to the economy. At the same time, the country's scarce aquifer-based water reserves have been depleting at astronomical rates to feed an unproductive drug habit that most Yemenis have, consuming a mildly stimulating narcotic leaf called khat. With oil revenues diminishing, water running out, and the country losing any capacity it may have to feed itself without foreign aid, Yemen is a nation at acute risk of economic collapse. When all of this is added to the gradual breakdown of law and order that is spreading across the country and to the aggressive secessionist movement in the south, it becomes clear that Yemen is well on its way to becoming a failed state.[1]

This failed state is one with a politically mobilized and heavily militarized citizenry organized around numerous insurgent groups that are competing for power and space and also looking to threaten Saudi Arabia. Today, the country is wracked by rebellion and insurgency, and the central government is unable to control even Sana'a, its capital. On one side is a rebellion by the Houthis, named for the founder of their movement, Hussein al-Houthi (d. 2004), and belonging to a Shia sect that is being courted by Iran. Between 2004 and 2010, the Houthis fought six wars with the central Yemeni government, and since the 2011 uprising against former President Ali Abdullah Saleh, they have "in effect run a state within a state" in the northwest province of Saada, which borders Saudi Arabia. Most recently, the Houthis succeeded in taking control of the Yemeni capital.[2]

The Iranians see their own advantage in creating a new hostile Shia front on Saudi Arabia's southern border, one that can work with them to undermine Saudi stability and

---

[1]   In 2013, Yemen was ranked the sixth most failed state in the world in the Failed States Index. See "Failed States: An Annual Report by FP and the Fund for Peace," *Foreign Policy*, accessed August 24, 2014, http://www.foreignpolicy.com/failedstates2013.

[2]   "Houthi Advance Changes Yemen's Political Dynamics," *The Economist* (July 15, 2014), accessed August 24, 2014, http://country.eiu.com/article.aspx?articleid=382020622&Country =Yemen&topic=Politics.

territorial integrity. Consequently, the Houthi rebels have been receiving military and financial support from the Iranians and are rapidly using this to take over wide swaths of Yemeni territory on Saudi Arabia's southwestern border. In 2012, unnamed US officials told the *New York Times* that "the Iranian aid to Yemen ... mirrors the kind of weapons and training the Quds Force is providing the embattled government of President Bashar al-Assad of Syria."[3] A "war" against these rebels in 2009 was an embarrassing failure for the Saudi military, which lost about a hundred soldiers and did little to damage the Houthi movement.[4]

In the rest of Yemen, extremist Sunni jihadist Islamism has been metastasizing for years. Successful antiterrorist efforts by the Saudi Ministry of Interior, after the bombings in Riyadh that followed 9/11, chased a lot of Saudi al-Qaeda operatives out of the country. They found a receptive new home in Yemen. Al-Qaeda in the Arabian Peninsula (AQAP) was then established as a merger between the Saudi and Yemeni branches of al-Qaeda and has been busy building up its network and capabilities since that time.

---

[3] Eric Schmitt and Robert F. Worth, "With Arms for Rebels, Iran Seeks Wider Mideast Role," *The New York Times* (March 15, 2012), accessed August 24, 2014, http://www.nytimes.com/2012/03/15/world/middleeast/aiding-yemen-rebels-iran-seeks-wider-mideast-role.html.

[4] Mohammed Aly Sergie, "Saudis Struggle in Battle with Rebels," *The Wall Street Journal* (January 20, 2010), accessed August 24, 2014, http://online.wsj.com/news/articles/SB10001424052748704561004575012792068180742.

Continued attempts by the Saudi and Yemeni govern-ments, with US military support and involvement through the drone program, have done little to arrest their growth. If anything, the US drone program has served only to publicly embarrass the Saudi government, as the Saudi opposition quickly took advantage of the inevitable leaks in the US media concerning this program, and the disclo-sure of the location of its base in southern Saudi Arabia on the Yemeni border, to accuse the Al Saud of "participating in the murder" of Muslims of Yemen.

All of this is taking place amid a background secessionist movement in South Yemen that is gaining traction. In May 2014, thousands of South Yemenis who feel politically and economical marginalized by the ruling North Yemenis demonstrated in the port city of Aden, chanting, "Twenty years of repression and resistance." They demanded inde-pendence, i.e., a return to the pre-1990 state of affairs when the two halves of the country were indeed separate.

On their own merit, Yemen's problems are worthy of a book, but the point here is to stress that Yemen's crisis will only overflow into Saudi Arabia—and nowhere else. Yemen is surrounded by the Indian Ocean and the Red Sea. Even its neighbors across the Red Sea, Somalia and Eritrea, are in very bad shape. This means that Saudi Arabia and, to a much lesser degree, Oman are the only countries to which Yemenis *can* escape, leaving their poverty and conflict behind.

Rather than attempting to create a permanent structural solution to this problem by fully opening GCC labor markets to Yemeni laborers, GCC governments are simply attempting to put up a virtual wall and isolate themselves from Yemen. In 2013, Saudi Arabia deported some two hundred thousand Yemeni laborers as a means of addressing its own unemployment issues.[5] It is also putting up a physical wall between itself and Yemen, constructing a thousand-mile border fence from the Red Sea to Oman.[6] Such a shortsighted policy will inevitably fail. In May of 2012, I published an article[7] calling for Yemen to be invited in as a full member of the GCC so as to allow the country's labor force free access to that market and also encourage GCC capital investment in Yemen. The reaction I got to that article from most of the GCC elites with whom I spoke afterwards was almost wholly negative. They were horrified at the idea of admitting millions of "poor Yemenis with guns" into their countries; this despite the presence of over ten million foreign laborers from countries as far away as India and the Philippines in these markets already, whose annual remittance earnings amount to billions of dollars. This remittance funding could instead end up in Yemen, stabilizing the country and giving its people a stake in a stable GCC. Now, as

---

[5] Abdulwahab Alkebsi, "Yemen and the GCC: Benefits of Labor Market Integration," *Foreign Policy* (November 8, 2013), accessed August 24, 2014, http://foreignpolicy.com/2013/11/08/yemen-and-the-gcc-benefits-of-labor-market-integration/.

[6] "Saudi Arabia Builds Giant Yemen Border Fence," *BBC* (April 9, 2013), accessed August 24, 2014, http://www.bbc.com/news/world-middle-east-22086231.

[7] The article is available at http://www.alishihabi.com/2012/05/case-for-yemen-joining-gcc.html.

Yemen's situation worsens by the day with the recent Houthi takeover of the capital (and maybe the state), the price of such short-term tactical thinking (at the expense of long-term strategy) becomes increasingly clear. It is, after all, ultimately easier to focus on the possible security problems that come with millions of Yemenis working in the GCC, most of whom will be gainfully employed and hence have a vested interest in their employers' well-being, rather than deal with the security nightmare that a collapse of the country will bring, not to mention the subsequent waves of angry, desperate, and militarized Yemenis pouring over the borders of the GCC.

Yemen will most likely crumble. As law and order break down, basic services break down, and poverty and desperation spread out among Yemen's population, a refugee crisis of immense proportions will emerge, driving millions of Yemenis over the fence and into Saudi Arabia. Nothing and no one will be able to stop them once they move. The potentially dire implications of this should be painfully obvious.[8]

---

[8] Stig Stenslie, "Not Too Strong, Not Too Weak: Saudi Arabia's Policy towards Yemen," *Norwegian Peacebuilding Resource Centre* (March 2013), accessed October 29, 2014, http://www.peacebuilding.no/var/ezflow_site/storage/original/application/87736bc4da8b0e482f9492e6e8baacaf.pdf. "A collapsed Yemen would lead to a surge in refugees crossing the border into Saudi Arabia, increased crime in the kingdom's southern provinces, primarily in the form of smuggling, and perhaps also piracy similar to that around Somalia," in addition to more jihadis using "the country as a safe haven and a platform for launching armed attacks in Saudi Arabia" and the Iranians buying greater "influence in the country."

CHAPTER 11

Conclusion: Ideas for Reform

Count Gabriel Honoré de Mirabeau, the greatest realist on the doctrines of the French Revolution, urged his king to lead the way for change, not combat it. "Sire," he argued, "the very idea of monarchy is not incompatible with revolution. Sire, abolish the privileges, modernize the state, and Your Majesty will come out stronger than before." How different history would have been had Louis listened to that wise prophet.[1]

—Erik Durschmied, *Blood of Revolution*

Political reform is always risky, and, as Alexis de Tocqueville so insightfully pointed out two centuries ago, an authoritarian government's most dangerous moment is when it attempts to reform. The understandable fear of such risks combined with a Saudi monarchy that instinctively tends toward inertia means that the default position is likely to continue to be perpetuation of the status quo.

---

[1] Erik Durschmied, *Blood of Revolution: From the Reign of Terror to the Rise of Khomeini* (New York: Arcade Publishing, 2003), 18–19.

For this inert Saudi attitude toward reform to be strategically sound and sustainable, however, the assumption has to be made that the Saudi people will continue to be docile and accept the dominance, across all facets of their life, of a large ruling class born to prominence, that anti-Saudi jihadi forces will be eliminated as a threat to the ruling order, that Iran will give up its geopolitical ambitions in Arabia, and that the Saudi Shia will reconcile themselves to their subservient status. It will also have to assume that what happens in Yemen stays in Yemen. While the probabilities associated with each of these threats can be debated endlessly, to expect *none* of them to materialize is clearly a tall order.

The only sustainable way that such threats can conceivably be overcome is by instituting reforms that strengthen the domestic political foundation of the Saudi state. Such reforms should focus on preserving, yet restructuring, the only two institutions (of governance) in existence today, the Al Saud and the Wahhabi establishment. It should redefine their roles to bring better governance, more justice, and increased transparency to the ruling order, rather than experiment with creating new political institutions.

The country is too fragile either to insert public participation (democracy) into the political process at this stage or to survive a removal of the House of Saud. Any attempt at regime change can only occur through violent revolution. There is no mechanism that can replace the Al Saud peacefully. They will certainly never step down voluntarily. At the same time, nobody, as far as I know, has been able to make a credible case for a successful scenario of peaceful transition from rule by the House of Saud to democracy and pluralism in the Arabian Peninsula. That is simply a pipe dream.

In a young polity like the Saudi state, the whole infrastructure of governance is tied so closely to the ruling family and dominated so completely by the Al Saud that no institution exists that could step in if the Al Saud were removed. Of course, the Al Saud are to blame for this, since they made certain that no independent institutions were allowed to develop within their borders. But this does not change the hard fact that the Al Saud today can quote Louis XV's famous statement "Après moi, le déluge"[2] with considerable credibility.

A paramount objective of any reform, under all circumstances, is to preserve the state's monopoly on violence and its infrastructure of governance—because, in young and underdeveloped states like Saudi Arabia, the decades of work to build this infrastructure can be blown away in days and then be impossible to rebuild in time to prevent complete state breakdown and failure. Time and again, we have seen this, most recently in Libya and even in Iraq. The modern Iraqi state's infrastructure of governance was basically destroyed by the US invasion of 2003. The Americans dissolved both the Baath Party and the Iraqi military, basically *the only two institutions of governance* in

---

2   Translated as, "After me, the flood [collapse]."

existence in Iraq at that time. As a result, basic governance—law and order and basic services—collapsed and had to be rebuilt. Ten years later, the government of Iraq is still unable to provide the elements of basic governance to all its people, despite not only the expenditure of hundreds of billions of dollars but also the active involvement of tens of thousands of US military personnel and civilian advisors at all levels of the Iraqi state.

Bearing the above points in mind, reform should prioritize steps to drastically reduce the size of the royal family. The current extended family needs to understand that their priority should be to preserve as much as is realistically possible of their wealth, social status, etc., rather than risk it all, including even their lives, by holding onto all royal privileges at any cost. They need to be reminded of the cruel outcome that history has always had in store for royals who failed to appreciate this point.

For Al Saud to take such a dramatic step, a strongman needs to emerge from within the family, a man who, like the late King Faisal, is able to force the rest of the family to accept change. While, ideally, the long-term goal should be to convert the royal succession into one based on primogeniture, an interim step could involve limiting princely titles to first- and second-generation descendants of King Abdul-Aziz and eliminating titles for those who come after. That step by itself would, over time, as these princes pass on, convert the royal family from the current tribe of thousands of princes to a small, manageable group. This, accompanied by reductions in the financial benefits and privileges available to royal family members, would go a long way in addressing this structural problem.

Reform should allow the Wahhabi establishment to regain its traditional independence from the monarchy and become the authority that checks and balances absolute monarchical power. This could involve, for example, giving the Wahhabis a key role to play in determining the monarchical succession. Today, this is something exclusively decided by the top members of Al Saud. Consent of the ulema is only obtained after the fact. Strengthening the only other institution of consequence in the country would conform to tradition and would productively utilize the ulema in carrying out the absolutely critical role of checking and balancing monarchical power. A check and balance on absolute power is absolutely essential for the long-term survival of any regime. In the kingdom today, the only immediately available institution that can carry out such a role is the Wahhabi ulema, whether one likes them or not.

While certainly no fan of this reactionary Wahhabi establishment, I recognize its entrenched role in Saudi society and the impossibility—and, in fact, the danger—of ignoring it. It is the only group other than the Al Saud that has any legitimacy with the people, along with the capacity and also the self-confidence to play such a vital role. While the current Wahhabi elderly leadership is increasingly discredited among the country's youth, more enlightened and independent elements among the ulema retain considerable credibility with the masses. They can play a constructive balancing role with the monarchy and, in turn, serve as an effective barrier against the more extreme jihadist elements that constitute a rapidly growing threat to stability. The quickly metastasizing jihadi threat fueled by the growing following of youth that radical extremist jihadi sheikhs are attracting can only be fought by setting against them more charismatic ulema who are not radical jihadis and who enjoy an independent and popular status among the people. It is only personalities like these who can beat the jihadis at their own game.

An idea here may be to replace the current crop of geriatric and reactionary members of the higher council of the ulema with younger and more charismatic individuals, people like Sheikh Salman al-Awda who have an independent attitude and an attractive and charismatic public persona that has allowed them to capture a wide following among the people. Such individuals should be able to restore to the Wahhabi establishment its stature and prestige with the common person and will also have the personality and courage to stand up to a king. This younger, media-savvy group of ulema are, by definition, much more attuned to the world around them. Well-traveled and well-read, they could become the agents of change to move this Wahhabi establishment forward and adapt it to the modern world. Again, everything here is relative. These people are obviously still Wahhabi scholars, not California liberals, but wise reform needs to accept this reality and work patiently with it.

In parallel, strengthening the independence of the judiciary, which would be evidenced by its willingness to subject the ruling elite to the rule of law as vigorously as it subjects the common person, is crucial to fortifying the legitimacy of Al Saud rule. A Saudi monarchy able to convince its people that it subjects every person, irrespective of his or her status, to the same standard of justice will win its people's continued loyalty.

Another important element of reform would be a much higher standard of government budgetary transparency. Corruption and the waste of oil revenue is a huge source of popular concern and dissatisfaction and, as discussed previously, is something that social media has increasingly allowed the opposition to expose. Budgetary transparency, where the government has to publicly disclose its revenues and expenditures in detail, would go a great way toward reducing the extensive corruption and waste that is currently practiced, by subjecting the government and specific individuals to public scrutiny and, ideally, legal oversight.

Finally, Saudi leaders urgently need to expose themselves to unfettered local public opinion. High-quality domestic political feedback and information, which the Saudi monarchy today lacks, is critical for effective governance. It is also a tool that can considerably increase the odds of the monarchy's survival. Saudi monarchs will only get this exposure if their people are allowed to freely express their opinions in the mainstream domestic media. It is certainly better for Saudi rulers to learn to endure a sometimes-hostile media that will alert them to hot-button issues, excesses by elites, mistakes in policy, and other problems that can be addressed in real time, rather than awake to such problems only when they explode into a crisis and come crashing through their palace doors. Today, the advent of social media has created a new space for the free expression of public opinion, which autocracies cannot control in any event. Extending this freedom to the mainstream local media will allow more moderate, but still credible, voices to balance the anti-government vitriol dominating the unruly social media space. It will also considerably increase the flow of reliable information available to a monarch and his key aides since they all avidly consume, sometimes exclusively, local media. Today, a Saudi monarch's only source of information on the health of his polity is his own bureaucracy. As has been recently seen with other autocracies—like that of Mubarak of Egypt, whose last message before his overthrow, from his minister of the interior, was one of reassurance that "all was under control"—such dependence can be fatal.

Over the past decades, Saudi Arabia has acquired a substantial, worldly, and sophisticated intellectual elite. More than half a century of mass education, hundreds of thousands of government-funded foreign scholarships, and decades of exposure to the outside world by this well-traveled segment of the population has created one of the more sophisticated intelligentsias in the Arab world today. An environment of freedom of speech that allows such elites to express their views via the media (and also within academia) would encourage this critically important element of society to participate constructively, albeit indirectly, in the governance of the country. It would also address the mounting resentment that these elites increasingly hold against the royals for monopolizing power and prominence. Failure to loosen the current government stranglehold on free speech will only drive more of these elites into opposition and possibly even radicalism.

A path to reform that uses the *existing* governing institutions in place today, namely the Al Saud and the Wahhabi ulema, rather than an approach that experiments with creating new institutions such as political parties, elected parliaments, etc., has the highest chance of success.

The outside stakeholders in Saudi stability—the United States and the industrialized world reliant on Saudi oil policy, and the Gulf Arab states that are attached at the hip to the Saudi state—should, to the extent that they have any influence, proactively encourage such reform.

The United States, in particular, should play a discreet leadership role in this effort. It should not underestimate its influence on the House of Saud and on Arabian elites in general. The elder generation of the Al Saud who grew up in a post-WWII environment where America was omnipotent instinctively attribute to the USA vast power and influence, something which American policy makers themselves may not feel they have. This attitude is even quite prevalent among the second generation of the royal family, so the Americans should take advantage of it, prodding and encouraging Saudi rulers to move forward with such reforms. Also, it is worth noting here that Arabian elites, in general, are more vulnerable to US pressure than many other third world elites are. Arabian elites are very plugged into the Western economic and social system since their lifestyles and their wealth have deep tentacles in the United States and Europe. They are unlike Iranian theocratic elites or the North Korean leadership, for example, who exist in isolated social and economic pockets at a remove from the wider world. Arabian elites are hooked on Western oxygen. They cannot operate without it.

While many will argue that the above reforms in and of themselves are impossible without democratic elections, I would point to the recent example of China, which has been gradually putting in place credible checks and balances within the ruling Communist Party. While this comparison is far from perfect, given the fact that the Chinese Communist Party is a far more meritocratic and competent ruling body than any ruling family defining its membership by blood can be, it still gives an example of how a non-democratic government can reform itself without introducing public political participation. The Chinese have come a long way in increasing the independence of their judiciary and subjecting their ruling elites to the full force of justice. China has also dramatically increased budgetary transparency across its many government entities and projects. Even freedom of speech, while hardly absolute, has greatly improved for the Chinese. Today's China is unquestionably a success story in

improving governance and reforming a totalitarian dictatorship without having to risk experimenting with
democracy. The Chinese model clearly provides examples
of the type of reform that the Al Saud can adopt.

In conclusion, it is critical that reform avoid the classical
trap of prioritizing process over outcome. In other words,
the focus should not be on *who* rules the country, but on *how*
the country is ruled. Rotating power among different
groups and elements of society is a luxury that only
advanced societies are realistically able to enjoy. In a young
country born out of the deserts of Arabia only decades ago,
the risks of experimenting with fundamental political
change now are just too great.

Clearly, any reform will certainly not be without risk, but
such risks are better taken soon, when they have a higher
chance of success, rather than later under the pressure of
domestic political turmoil, when reforms end up being
seen by opponents as a sign of weakness and then only
accelerate state breakdown. As Gustave Le Bon points out
in his classic *The Psychology of Revolution*[3] (written a century
after the French Revolution), commenting on the nobility's
willingness to finally give up their privileges as the revolution was unfolding,

> If the renunciation of their rights had been effected by
> the nobility a few years earlier, the Revolution would

---

[3]   Gustave Le Bon, *The Psychology of Revolution* (originally published in
      1913), trans. Bernard Miall (Kitchener, Ontario: Batoche Books, 2001),
      101.

doubtless have been avoided, but it was now too late. To give way only when one is forced to do so merely increases the demands of those to whom one yields. *In politics one should always look ahead and give way long before one is forced to do so* [author's emphasis].

Today, the Saudi state faces acute and imminent existential threats. These threats require an alert, bold, and proactive leadership that has the vision and courage to implement deep structural reforms that address these fundamental risks and threats, rather than a leadership that continues to react tactically. What Saudi Arabia needs is leadership that is willing to perform surgery rather than apply simple Band-Aids—and it needs this leadership yesterday. Failure to meet this challenge will have tragic implications for the country and for other Arab Gulf states and will cause massive damage to the world economy.

POSTSCRIPT

The ascendancy of King Salman bin Abdulaziz to the throne, just as this book goes to press, and the unexpected and welcome appointment of Prince Muhammad bin Nayef as Deputy Crown Prince, secure the line of royal succession very clearly and decisively. It also brings to power a team with the prestige and capability to address the pressing issues discussed in this book.

Lightning Source UK Ltd.
Milton Keynes UK
UKOW02n1339170415

249844UK00002B/5/P